# THE BIG DATA REVOLUTION

## Harness the Power of Big Data with Modern Tools and Technologies

# THOMPSON CARTER

# TABLE OF CONTENTS

# Introduction

*Big Data: Unlocking Insights from the Digital Age*

In the digital age, data has become one of the most valuable assets for businesses, governments, and individuals alike. The rise of connected devices, social media, e-commerce, and the Internet of Things (IoT) has led to an explosion of data, commonly referred to as **big data**. With the ability to process, analyze, and extract valuable insights from vast amounts of information, big data is reshaping industries, improving decision-making, and driving innovation across the globe.

This book, ***Big Data: Unlocking Insights from the Digital Age***, serves as a comprehensive guide to understanding, working with, and leveraging big data. Whether you're a business professional, a data scientist, a student, or an enthusiast eager to understand the growing influence of big data, this book provides the knowledge, tools, and real-world applications to help you navigate this evolving field.

---

### *What is Big Data?*

Big data refers to datasets that are so large, fast-moving, or complex that they cannot be managed, processed, or analyzed using traditional methods or software tools. Big data is often characterized by the **three Vs**:

- **Volume**: The massive amount of data generated every second—from social media posts to sensor readings from IoT devices.
- **Velocity**: The speed at which data is generated and needs to be processed in real time or near real time.
- **Variety**: The different types of data that exist, including structured data (e.g., databases), semi-structured data (e.g., XML files), and unstructured data (e.g., images, videos, and social media posts).

Beyond the traditional three Vs, big data can also be analyzed through the **fourth V—Veracity** (the uncertainty or quality of the data), and the **fifth V—Value** (the usefulness of the data).

In a world where data flows continuously from millions of sources, the ability to manage, analyze, and derive actionable insights from big data is crucial for success. This book delves into how big data is transforming various sectors, providing a deeper understanding of the tools, technologies, and techniques that enable businesses and individuals to extract meaningful insights from these massive datasets.

## *Why Big Data Matters*

Big data is not just a buzzword—it's a revolution that is reshaping industries, enhancing business operations, and solving global challenges. As the amount of data generated each day grows exponentially, the importance of understanding and utilizing this resource cannot be overstated.

- **In Healthcare**: Big data enables better patient care, more effective treatments, and predictive analytics that can prevent disease outbreaks and improve overall health outcomes.
- **In Finance**: Financial institutions use big data for fraud detection, algorithmic trading, customer segmentation, and risk management, giving them a competitive edge.
- **In E-commerce**: Retailers leverage big data to personalize shopping experiences, optimize inventory management, and improve supply chain logistics.
- **In Government and Public Sector**: Big data helps governments make more informed decisions, enhance public services, and manage resources more effectively.

At its core, big data empowers organizations to make data-driven decisions. The ability to analyze vast quantities of data leads to improved insights, better business strategies, and innovative products and services.

*What You Will Learn*

This book is structured to guide you through the journey of understanding big data, from its foundational concepts to its advanced applications. Each chapter is designed to build on the previous one, offering a comprehensive approach to learning how to harness the power of big data.

1. **Introduction to Big Data**: You will begin with a solid foundation in what big data is, its characteristics, and how it differs from traditional data.

2. **Big Data Technologies**: The book covers the essential technologies used to store, process, and analyze big data, including **Hadoop**, **Apache Spark**, **NoSQL databases**, and more.

3. **Data Processing and Analysis**: Learn about data preprocessing, the importance of data cleaning, and how to implement powerful data analysis methods, including machine learning and artificial intelligence.

4. **Real-World Applications**: The book dives deep into case studies across industries such as healthcare, finance, e-commerce, and government, showing how big data is used to solve real-world problems and drive business success.

5. **Ethics and Bias in Big Data**: Understand the ethical implications of collecting and using big data, and learn how to address issues such as bias in data models and algorithms.

6. **The Future of Big Data**: The book concludes with insights into the emerging trends shaping the future of big data, including **quantum computing, AI, edge computing**, and **sustainability**.

---

## *For Whom This Book is Intended*

This book is for anyone looking to understand and work with big data:

- **Business Professionals**: If you are a decision-maker, manager, or entrepreneur, this book will help you understand how big data can improve your business operations, enhance customer experiences, and optimize resource management.

- **Data Scientists and Analysts**: If you are involved in data analysis or data science, you'll gain a thorough understanding of the tools and techniques used to work with big data, from data collection and processing to advanced analytics and machine learning.

- **Students and Beginners**: For those new to the field of big data, this book provides a comprehensive, jargon-free approach that builds a solid foundation for future learning and exploration.

- **Tech Enthusiasts**: If you are fascinated by the future of technology and want to understand how big data is driving innovation, this book will provide valuable insights into the latest trends and tools in the field.

---

### Real-World Examples and Case Studies

Throughout this book, we emphasize **real-world examples** and **case studies** to illustrate how big data is applied in various industries. From **predictive maintenance** in manufacturing to **personalized marketing** in e-commerce, the examples are designed to show you how big data can be practically applied to solve problems and create value in the real world.

Each chapter is designed to take you through the journey of not only understanding the theoretical aspects of big data but also applying these concepts in a practical setting. Whether it's building a big data pipeline or using machine learning models for data analysis, you'll gain hands-on experience that you can apply immediately.

---

*Big Data: Unlocking Insights from the Digital Age* is your gateway to understanding how big data is transforming the world.

Whether you're looking to use big data to drive business success, gain new insights into healthcare, or explore its potential in sustainability, this book offers the knowledge, tools, and resources you need to get started.

By the end of this book, you will have a comprehensive understanding of the **technologies, tools**, and **techniques** behind big data. You will be equipped with the skills to work with big data in various applications, from **data storage** and **processing** to **analysis** and **visualization**. With **practical case studies, real-world examples**, and a deep dive into **emerging trends**, this book is your essential resource for navigating the rapidly evolving world of big data.

# Chapter 1: Introduction to Big Data

Big data is one of the most transformative phenomena of the 21st century, and its impact is being felt across every industry. As the amount of data being generated continues to increase exponentially, the ability to capture, store, process, and analyze this data has become a critical driver of innovation, productivity, and competitiveness. This chapter serves as an introduction to **big data**, explaining what it is, why it matters, and how it is reshaping industries. We will also explore the **5 V's of Big Data—Volume, Velocity, Variety, Veracity,** and **Value**—as fundamental characteristics that define this vast and complex landscape. Finally, we will look at a **real-world example** of how big data is revolutionizing **healthcare** and improving patient care.

---

### *Defining Big Data: What is Big Data and Why Does it Matter?*

**Big data** refers to datasets that are so large and complex that traditional data processing tools and methods can no longer handle them efficiently. Unlike smaller datasets, which can be analyzed using conventional tools like spreadsheets and databases, big data requires specialized technologies and frameworks to store, manage, and process it. Big data can come from a variety of sources, including social media, sensors, machine logs, customer transactions, and much more.

What makes big data particularly valuable is not just the sheer size of the data, but the ability to extract insights from it that would otherwise remain hidden. By analyzing large volumes of data, organizations can:

- Uncover hidden patterns and trends.
- Make more informed decisions.
- Predict future events or behaviors.
- Optimize processes and improve performance.

The importance of big data lies in its potential to drive decision-making, innovation, and competitive advantage. Businesses, governments, healthcare providers, and researchers are increasingly relying on big data to gain insights that were previously inaccessible, ultimately leading to better outcomes and solutions.

---

### The 5 V's of Big Data: Volume, Velocity, Variety, Veracity, and Value

The **5 V's** of big data are key characteristics that define the challenges and opportunities presented by large datasets. Each "V" represents a dimension of big data that organizations must address in order to effectively manage and utilize it:

1. Volume

- **Volume** refers to the vast amount of data being generated every second. This can range from petabytes (1,000 terabytes) to exabytes (1 million terabytes) of data. For example, social media platforms like Facebook and Twitter generate terabytes of data daily from user interactions, posts, and messages. Managing and storing this enormous volume of data is one of the core challenges of big data.

## 2. Velocity

- **Velocity** is the speed at which data is generated, processed, and analyzed. In today's world, data is produced at an unprecedented rate, requiring real-time or near-real-time processing to extract insights. For instance, in financial markets, millions of transactions are made every second, and timely analysis is crucial for decision-making. Streaming data from sensors, online activity, and social media further emphasizes the need for fast data processing.

## 3. Variety

- **Variety** refers to the different types of data—structured, semi-structured, and unstructured. Data can come in many forms, including:
  - **Structured data**: Data that fits neatly into rows and columns (e.g., spreadsheets or relational databases).

○ **Semi-structured data**: Data with a loosely defined structure, such as JSON files or XML.

○ **Unstructured data**: Data that has no predefined format, like social media posts, images, videos, and sensor data.

The variety of data types presents challenges for data integration, processing, and analysis, requiring sophisticated tools that can handle different formats simultaneously.

## 4. Veracity

- **Veracity** refers to the reliability, accuracy, and quality of the data. Big data can be noisy, incomplete, or inconsistent, which can impact the accuracy of insights derived from it. For example, social media data may contain false information or incomplete data, and sensor data may have errors or discrepancies. Ensuring data quality is critical for making valid predictions and drawing meaningful s.

## 5. Value

- **Value** is perhaps the most important aspect of big data. It's not enough to simply collect large amounts of data—organizations must be able to extract actionable insights from it. This can involve identifying trends, making predictions, or discovering hidden patterns that drive business or societal value. The real challenge lies in transforming raw data into valuable insights that improve decision-making and provide a competitive edge.

---

### *How Big Data is Transforming Industries*

Big data is having a profound impact across various industries, revolutionizing how organizations operate, make decisions, and deliver products and services. Here are some examples of how big data is transforming key sectors:

## 1. Healthcare

- Big data is enabling healthcare providers to offer more personalized care, predict patient outcomes, and optimize hospital operations. By analyzing patient data, medical records, wearables, and genetic information, healthcare providers can improve diagnostics, treatment plans, and patient monitoring. Predictive models powered by big data can help detect diseases earlier, leading to better outcomes.

## 2. Finance

- The financial industry uses big data for fraud detection, risk management, and algorithmic trading. By analyzing large amounts of transactional data, financial institutions can spot suspicious activity in real-time, mitigate risks, and improve decision-making. Big data also enables personalized banking services, tailored to individual customers' preferences and behaviors.

## 3. Retail

- Retailers use big data to understand consumer behavior, personalize shopping experiences, optimize inventory management, and predict future demand. By analyzing transactional data, social media interactions, and website activity, retailers can target customers with relevant products, promotions, and recommendations, improving sales and customer satisfaction.

## 4. Manufacturing

- In manufacturing, big data is used for predictive maintenance, supply chain optimization, and improving production efficiency. By analyzing sensor data from machines, manufacturers can predict when equipment will fail, allowing for timely repairs and minimizing downtime. Additionally, big data helps optimize production processes, reducing waste and improving quality.

## 5. Transportation and Logistics

- Big data is being used to optimize traffic management, improve logistics, and enhance route planning. By analyzing GPS data, traffic patterns, and weather forecasts, cities can reduce congestion, improve public transportation efficiency, and enhance delivery times for logistics companies.

---

### Real-World Example: Big Data in Healthcare (Improving Patient Care)

One of the most compelling examples of big data's potential is its application in the **healthcare industry**, where it is helping to improve patient care, reduce costs, and enhance overall healthcare delivery. By leveraging vast amounts of health data—from electronic health records (EHRs) and medical imaging to wearable devices and genomics—healthcare professionals can gain a deeper understanding of patient conditions and treatment efficacy.

### Example: Predicting Disease Outbreaks and Personalized Treatment

- Healthcare providers and researchers are using big data to analyze patterns in patient symptoms, treatment outcomes, and population health data. For instance, by analyzing vast datasets of patient records, public health organizations can predict disease outbreaks or track the spread of illnesses like the flu, COVID-19, or malaria in real time.

**Personalized Medicine**: Big data enables the development of personalized treatment plans. By analyzing genetic data, lifestyle factors, and clinical history, doctors can tailor treatments to individual patients. This is particularly valuable in oncology, where big data helps identify the best course of treatment for different types of cancer based on genetic profiles.

**Wearables and Remote Monitoring**: Devices like fitness trackers and smartwatches collect real-time data on patients' heart rates, sleep patterns, activity levels, and more. This data can be analyzed to detect early signs of health issues, enabling early intervention and personalized health advice.

In this chapter, we introduced **big data**—what it is, why it matters, and how it is revolutionizing industries across the globe. We explored the **5 V's of Big Data**: **Volume**, **Velocity**, **Variety**, **Veracity**, and **Value**, which are the key dimensions that define big data and its challenges. Big data is enabling transformative changes in sectors such as healthcare, finance, retail, and manufacturing, and its potential is only beginning to be realized.

We also discussed a **real-world example** of how big data is improving patient care in the healthcare industry by enabling better diagnostics, personalized treatments, and early disease detection. As big data continues to evolve, its applications will only expand, offering new opportunities for innovation and improved outcomes across all sectors.

In the following chapters, we will dive deeper into the tools, technologies, and techniques used to process, analyze, and extract insights from big data, starting with how we collect and store large datasets and the technologies that power big data analytics.

# Chapter 2: The Evolution of Big Data

Big data has become one of the most influential forces driving technological and business innovation in the modern world. However, its rise has been gradual, evolving over decades as the amount of data generated and the technologies to process it have advanced. This chapter will explore the **evolution of big data**, examining the journey from **small data** to **big data**, key milestones in the **big data revolution**, and how **technology** has enabled the big data era. We will also take a close look at a **real-world example** of how big data has transformed the **retail industry**, particularly in the area of **personalized shopping experiences**.

---

### *The Journey from Small Data to Big Data*

Before the emergence of big data, the term "data" referred to relatively small datasets that could be easily managed, stored, and analyzed with traditional tools like spreadsheets and relational databases. These smaller datasets were often static, structured, and easy to process, and were typically analyzed using traditional **statistical methods**.

However, the rapid increase in the amount of data being generated—due to advances in technology, the internet, and the rise of social media—has led to the growth of **big data**. Big data differs from small data in several key ways:

## 1. Volume

- **Small data** refers to datasets that are relatively small and manageable, often fitting within the memory of a single computer or database. These datasets are easy to store, process, and analyze using traditional tools and methods.
- **Big data**, on the other hand, refers to datasets that are so large and complex that they require specialized tools and technologies to process. These datasets often exceed the storage capacity of traditional systems and are distributed across multiple machines or even data centers.

## 2. Velocity

- Small data was often generated slowly, with a manageable pace of collection and processing.
- Big data is generated at an unprecedented speed, with real-time or near-real-time data being collected from a variety of sources such as social media, sensors, transactions, and more.

## 3. Variety

- Small data typically comes in structured formats, such as tables with rows and columns, and is easy to manage.
- Big data includes a variety of formats, such as structured, semi-structured, and unstructured data. This includes text,

images, video, social media posts, sensor data, and more, making it much more challenging to process and analyze.

---

### *Key Milestones in the Big Data Revolution*

The evolution of big data has been shaped by key milestones in both technology and data-driven thinking. These milestones have transformed how we generate, store, process, and analyze data, allowing for the widespread adoption of big data across industries.

1. The Rise of the Internet and the Digital Revolution

- The internet played a pivotal role in the explosion of data. As more people, businesses, and devices went online, massive amounts of data began to be generated. Every click, transaction, and interaction produced valuable data that could be collected, stored, and analyzed.
- The digital revolution, fueled by the widespread adoption of personal computers, mobile phones, and online platforms, laid the foundation for the big data era.

2. The Introduction of Cloud Computing

- Cloud computing, starting in the early 2000s, allowed businesses to scale their storage and computing resources without having to maintain expensive hardware. Cloud platforms like **Amazon Web Services (AWS)** and

**Microsoft Azure** revolutionized big data by making it more affordable and accessible.

- Cloud computing enabled organizations to store vast amounts of data without worrying about infrastructure, and it allowed for the processing of this data using distributed systems.

## 3. The Emergence of Big Data Technologies

- In the mid-2000s, **Apache Hadoop** was introduced, revolutionizing big data storage and processing. Hadoop's distributed file system (HDFS) allowed businesses to store data across multiple machines, while the **MapReduce** framework enabled large-scale parallel processing.
- In 2010, **Apache Spark** emerged as a faster alternative to Hadoop, capable of performing in-memory computations and real-time analytics, further accelerating big data processing.

## 4. The Age of Machine Learning and AI

- As big data grew, the need for more advanced analytics emerged. **Machine learning** and **artificial intelligence (AI)** algorithms became integral to extracting valuable insights from big data.
- Technologies such as **deep learning**, **natural language processing (NLP)**, and **computer vision** began to leverage

big data to automate decision-making and create new innovations, such as autonomous vehicles, facial recognition systems, and personalized recommendations.

---

### *How Technology Has Enabled the Big Data Era*

Technology has played a key role in enabling the big data revolution, providing the infrastructure, tools, and methodologies needed to handle large and complex datasets. The following technological advancements have been instrumental in making big data a reality:

#### 1. Data Storage and Distributed Systems

- Traditional databases could not handle the sheer scale and complexity of big data. Distributed systems like **Hadoop** and **NoSQL databases** (e.g., **MongoDB**, **Cassandra**) provided scalable solutions for storing and managing large datasets. These systems can spread data across multiple machines, allowing for more efficient storage and processing.
- **Cloud storage** solutions, such as AWS S3 and Google Cloud Storage, have made it easier and more cost-effective for businesses to store vast amounts of data.

#### 2. Data Processing Frameworks

- **MapReduce**, introduced by Google, was a breakthrough for processing large datasets in parallel across distributed systems. **Hadoop** adopted this framework, enabling the processing of massive datasets.

- **Apache Spark** provided a significant improvement over Hadoop by allowing for faster in-memory processing. This made real-time data analytics possible, which is essential for applications like fraud detection, social media sentiment analysis, and dynamic pricing.

## 3. Real-Time Data Processing

- Technologies like **Apache Kafka** and **Apache Flink** allowed organizations to process real-time streams of data, enabling faster decision-making and automation. These tools are essential for applications that require immediate responses, such as detecting anomalies in financial transactions or monitoring traffic in smart cities.

## 4. Machine Learning and AI Integration

- Machine learning frameworks like **TensorFlow**, **PyTorch**, and **scikit-learn** have enabled big data to be analyzed using sophisticated algorithms. These frameworks allow for automated insights, predictions, and decision-making, turning big data into actionable intelligence.

## 5. Data Visualization Tools

- **Tableau**, **Power BI**, and other data visualization platforms allow data scientists and business leaders to visualize complex big data insights. These tools help make data more accessible and easier to interpret, driving business decisions and innovation.

---

*Real-World Example: Big Data's Impact on Retail (Personalized Shopping Experiences)*

One of the most prominent applications of big data is in the **retail industry**, where data is used to personalize shopping experiences, optimize inventory management, and improve customer engagement.

1. Personalizing the Customer Experience

Retailers are using big data to analyze customer behavior and tailor their offerings. By analyzing purchase history, browsing patterns, and customer demographics, companies can provide personalized product recommendations and discounts that appeal to individual preferences. This personalization leads to increased customer satisfaction and loyalty.

For example, **Amazon** uses big data to recommend products based on users' past purchases, searches, and interactions with the platform. The more a customer interacts with the platform, the more refined and personalized the recommendations become.

## 2. Optimizing Pricing and Inventory Management

Big data is also helping retailers optimize pricing strategies. By analyzing data on customer demand, competitor pricing, and market trends, retailers can adjust their prices in real-time to maximize sales and profit. Dynamic pricing models enable retailers to offer discounts or adjust prices based on factors such as time of day, demand, and inventory levels.

Similarly, retailers use big data to optimize inventory management. By analyzing sales trends, stock levels, and seasonal patterns, retailers can forecast demand more accurately, reducing waste and ensuring popular products are always in stock.

## 3. Improving Marketing and Customer Engagement

Big data enables more targeted marketing campaigns. By analyzing social media activity, purchase history, and browsing behavior, retailers can create highly personalized marketing messages that resonate with their target audience. This leads to more effective advertising and higher conversion rates.

For example, **Target** has famously used predictive analytics to identify patterns in consumer behavior, leading to personalized marketing campaigns and promotions that increase customer engagement and sales.

In this chapter, we explored the **evolution of big data**, from the early days of small data to the vast, complex datasets that define the modern world. We discussed the **5 V's** of big data—**Volume, Velocity, Variety, Veracity**, and **Value**—as key characteristics that differentiate big data from traditional datasets. We also examined how advancements in **cloud computing, distributed storage, real-time processing**, and **machine learning** have enabled the big data era.

The **real-world example** of big data in retail highlighted how companies are using big data to **personalize shopping experiences, optimize pricing and inventory**, and **engage customers** more effectively.

As big data continues to evolve, it will play an even more critical role in shaping industries, transforming business practices, and driving innovation. In the upcoming chapters, we will dive deeper into the tools, technologies, and methodologies that enable the management, processing, and analysis of big data.

# Chapter 3: The Big Data Ecosystem

In this chapter, we will explore the **big data ecosystem**—a collection of tools, technologies, and practices that work together to enable the storage, processing, and analysis of massive datasets. Understanding this ecosystem is essential for anyone seeking to leverage big data for decision-making and innovation. We will also dive into **data storage solutions**, focusing on the differences between **data lakes** and **data warehouses**, and explore a **real-world example** of how big data is used in the **finance industry**, particularly in **fraud detection**.

---

### *Overview of the Big Data Ecosystem: Tools and Technologies*

The big data ecosystem includes a wide range of tools and technologies designed to handle the various challenges of managing large datasets. These technologies span from data collection and storage to processing, analysis, and visualization. The key components of the big data ecosystem are as follows:

### 1. Data Collection

- **Data Collection** is the first step in the big data process, and it involves gathering data from multiple sources such as IoT devices, social media, transactions, sensors, and more. Popular tools for data collection include:

- ○ **Apache Kafka**: A distributed streaming platform used for real-time data collection and processing.
- ○ **Apache Flume**: A service for collecting, aggregating, and moving large amounts of data, often used for log data.
- ○ **Logstash**: A tool for collecting, parsing, and forwarding logs and other event data to a central system.

## 2. Data Storage

Big data storage solutions must be scalable, flexible, and capable of handling vast amounts of data. Two of the primary storage paradigms are **data lakes** and **data warehouses**:

- **Data Lakes**: A storage repository that can hold vast amounts of raw, unstructured, semi-structured, and structured data. Data lakes are ideal for storing all types of data, including log files, multimedia, and sensor data.
- **Data Warehouses**: A structured repository used for storing and analyzing processed data. Data warehouses use predefined schemas and are optimized for query performance.

## 3. Data Processing

Big data processing frameworks allow for the **parallel processing** of data across multiple machines. These tools are essential for transforming raw data into useful insights.

- **Apache Hadoop**: A framework that enables the distributed storage and processing of large datasets using the **MapReduce** programming model.
- **Apache Spark**: An alternative to Hadoop, Spark is faster and supports real-time processing, machine learning, and SQL-based queries.
- **Apache Flink**: A stream processing framework used for real-time data analysis and event-driven applications.

## 4. Data Analytics

- **Machine Learning**: Once data is processed, machine learning algorithms can be applied to identify patterns, make predictions, and derive insights from the data. Tools like **TensorFlow**, **PyTorch**, and **scikit-learn** are commonly used for machine learning applications on big data.
- **Business Intelligence (BI)**: BI tools like **Tableau**, **Power BI**, and **Qlik** enable users to visualize data and perform advanced analytics to support decision-making.

## 5. Data Visualization

- **Data visualization** is essential for making sense of big data. Tools like **D3.js**, **Matplotlib**, and **Plotly** help create interactive and static visualizations, allowing decision-makers to easily interpret complex data patterns.

## 6. Cloud Platforms

- The rise of cloud computing has significantly facilitated big data management. Cloud platforms like **Amazon Web Services (AWS)**, **Google Cloud**, and **Microsoft Azure** offer services for data storage, processing, and analysis at scale.

---

### *Data Storage Solutions: Data Lakes vs. Data Warehouses*

The distinction between **data lakes** and **data warehouses** is fundamental when discussing big data storage solutions. Both serve the purpose of storing large amounts of data, but they are designed for different use cases.

## 1. Data Lakes

- **What is a Data Lake?** A **data lake** is a centralized repository that stores **raw** data in its native format. Data lakes can handle large volumes of structured, semi-structured, and unstructured data, such as log files, social media posts, sensor readings, and multimedia content.

- **Advantages of Data Lakes**:
  - **Flexibility**: Data lakes can store virtually any type of data, including text, images, videos, and sensor data.
  - **Scalability**: Data lakes can scale easily to handle petabytes or more of data.
  - **Cost-effective**: Since data lakes store raw data, they tend to be less expensive than traditional relational databases.
- **Disadvantages**:
  - **Data Quality**: Since data lakes store unprocessed data, there can be issues with data quality, consistency, and structure.
  - **Data Governance**: Managing and governing raw data in a data lake can be complex, requiring robust data cataloging and management practices.
- **Common Use Cases**:
  - Storing large volumes of **IoT sensor data** for analysis.
  - Aggregating **social media data** for sentiment analysis.
  - **Real-time data streaming** from various sources.

## 2. Data Warehouses

- **What is a Data Warehouse?** A **data warehouse** is a structured repository designed to store processed and cleaned data. Unlike data lakes, data warehouses use **predefined schemas** (e.g., star or snowflake schemas) and are optimized for performing **complex queries** and **analytics**.

- **Advantages of Data Warehouses**:
  - o **Fast Query Performance**: Data warehouses are designed for complex queries and aggregations, making them ideal for business intelligence applications.
  - o **Data Consistency**: Since data is cleaned and processed before being loaded into a data warehouse, it tends to be more consistent and accurate.

- **Disadvantages**:
  - o **Limited Data Types**: Data warehouses primarily handle **structured** data. Unstructured or semi-structured data is not easily accommodated.
  - o **Cost**: Data warehouses can be more expensive to implement and maintain, especially as data volumes grow.

- **Common Use Cases**:
  - o **Business Intelligence (BI)** applications, where fast and consistent query performance is needed.
  - o **Financial analytics**, where data from multiple sources is integrated and analyzed for reporting.

o **Sales and marketing analytics**, where structured data such as customer information and transactional data is analyzed.

**Key Differences Between Data Lakes and Data Warehouses**

| Aspect | Data Lake | Data Warehouse |
|---|---|---|
| **Data Type** | Raw, unstructured, semi-structured, structured | Processed, structured |
| **Storage Format** | Native format (JSON, CSV, Avro, Parquet) | Structured data (tables) |
| **Processing** | Batch or real-time processing | Optimized for batch processing |
| **Scalability** | Highly scalable for massive data sets | Scalable but can be more expensive |
| **Cost** | More cost-effective for large data volumes | Can be more costly due to data processing |

*Real-World Example: Big Data in Finance (Fraud Detection)*
One of the most impactful applications of big data is in the **finance industry**, where big data is leveraged for **fraud detection**. Financial institutions process billions of transactions daily, and analyzing this

data in real-time is crucial for identifying fraudulent activities. Big data technologies and machine learning models are enabling banks and financial institutions to detect fraud faster and more accurately than ever before.

## How Big Data is Used in Fraud Detection

1. **Data Collection**: Financial institutions collect vast amounts of data from various sources, such as customer transactions, online banking activities, credit card usage, and customer behavior. This data is often unstructured (e.g., clickstreams, email exchanges) or semi-structured (e.g., transaction logs), making it ideal for storage in a **data lake**.

2. **Data Processing and Analysis**: Using **Apache Kafka** and **Apache Flink**, financial institutions can process data in real-time to detect anomalous patterns in customer behavior. For example, if a customer's account experiences an unusually high number of transactions or withdrawals in a short time, it may trigger an alert for potential fraud.

3. **Machine Learning Models**: Machine learning algorithms are employed to analyze historical transaction data and learn patterns of normal behavior. Once trained, these models can predict whether a new transaction is fraudulent based on known features such as:

   o **Geographical location** of the transaction.

- o **Transaction amount** relative to the customer's average spend.
- o **Frequency** of transactions in a short period.

4. **Real-Time Detection**: By using **Apache Spark** and **Hadoop**, financial institutions can analyze streaming data and provide near-instant alerts for potentially fraudulent transactions. If the system detects suspicious activity, it can automatically block the transaction and notify the customer or security team.

## Impact of Big Data on Fraud Detection

- **Speed**: Big data tools allow financial institutions to process and analyze vast amounts of transaction data in real-time, enabling them to detect fraud as it happens.
- **Accuracy**: Machine learning models trained on big data can identify subtle patterns and anomalies that traditional methods might miss, improving the accuracy of fraud detection.
- **Cost Savings**: By detecting fraud early, financial institutions can prevent financial losses and reduce the cost of fraud investigation and mitigation.

In this chapter, we explored the **big data ecosystem**, focusing on the core tools and technologies that enable the management, processing, and analysis of vast amounts of data. We also examined the fundamental differences between **data lakes** and **data warehouses**, two key storage solutions in the big data landscape. Understanding these solutions helps organizations determine how to best store and manage their data based on their needs.

We concluded with a **real-world example** of how big data is transforming the **finance industry** through **fraud detection**. By harnessing the power of big data, financial institutions can analyze vast datasets in real-time, detect fraud more accurately, and improve customer security.

As we continue in this book, we will delve deeper into the tools, frameworks, and best practices for working with big data, and explore how industries beyond finance, such as healthcare, retail, and manufacturing, are also leveraging big data for innovation and growth.

# Chapter 4: Data Collection Methods

Data collection is the first crucial step in the **big data pipeline**. The insights derived from big data depend heavily on how the data is collected, and in today's interconnected world, there are countless sources and methods for gathering data. In this chapter, we will explore how big data is collected from various sources, including **sensors**, **social media**, **web scraping**, **APIs**, and **IoT devices**. We will also dive into the significance of **real-time data collection** and provide a **real-world example** of how data collection is utilized in **smart cities**.

---

*How Big Data is Collected: From Sensors to Social Media*

## 1. Sensors: Collecting Data from the Physical World

Sensors are devices that capture data from the environment, transforming real-world phenomena into digital data. These devices can measure temperature, humidity, motion, pressure, sound, and even biological signals. Sensors are integral to many industries, including manufacturing, transportation, healthcare, and agriculture.

- **Applications of Sensors**:
    - **Industrial Monitoring**: Sensors in factories can monitor machinery for signs of wear and tear,

triggering maintenance before equipment failure occurs.

- ○ **Agriculture**: Soil moisture sensors in farms collect data on irrigation needs, optimizing water usage and crop yield.
- ○ **Healthcare**: Wearable sensors track vital signs such as heart rate, sleep patterns, and activity levels in real-time, providing valuable data for health monitoring.

- **Challenges**: Data collection through sensors often involves large volumes of continuous, real-time data, which must be stored, processed, and analyzed efficiently. The diversity of sensor types and the format of the collected data adds complexity to managing sensor data.

## 2. Social Media: Harvesting User-Generated Data

Social media platforms, such as **Facebook**, **Twitter**, **Instagram**, and **YouTube**, generate vast amounts of unstructured data. This data includes user posts, comments, likes, shares, videos, and other forms of interactions. Analyzing this data allows companies to gain insights into customer sentiment, market trends, and consumer behavior.

- **Applications of Social Media Data**:

- o **Sentiment Analysis**: Analyzing user comments and posts to gauge public opinion on brands, products, or political events.

- o **Market Research**: Tracking the popularity of certain topics, hashtags, or products based on social media mentions.

- o **Influencer Marketing**: Identifying and analyzing the impact of social media influencers on consumer behavior.

- **Challenges**: Social media data is largely unstructured and contains a high level of noise. Parsing and analyzing this data in a meaningful way requires sophisticated natural language processing (NLP) techniques.

---

## *Web Scraping and APIs*

### 1. Web Scraping: Extracting Data from Websites

Web scraping is a method used to collect data from websites by extracting content from HTML pages. This technique allows data scientists and businesses to gather information such as prices, product reviews, news articles, and more from publicly accessible websites.

- **How Web Scraping Works**:

- A web scraper sends HTTP requests to web pages, then extracts relevant data from the HTML, typically through techniques like **XPath** or **CSS selectors**.

- The extracted data is stored in a structured format, such as **CSV**, **JSON**, or a database, for further analysis.

- **Applications of Web Scraping**:
    - **Price Comparison**: Collecting pricing data from various e-commerce sites to compare products and optimize pricing strategies.
    - **Market Research**: Scraping reviews, forums, and blogs to gather customer feedback and sentiment.
    - **Real-Time Stock Market Data**: Collecting financial data, news, and stock prices from multiple sources to inform trading decisions.

- **Challenges**: Some websites may block or limit access to their content, and scraping large amounts of data without permission can raise ethical and legal concerns. Additionally, the structure of websites changes frequently, requiring scrapers to be updated regularly.

## 2. APIs (Application Programming Interfaces): Structured Data Access

APIs are another method of collecting data, providing a structured way for applications to communicate and share information. Many websites, social media platforms, and services provide APIs that allow developers to access specific data points programmatically.

- **Examples of Popular APIs**:
  - o **Twitter API**: Provides access to tweet data, user information, and trends.
  - o **Google Maps API**: Allows businesses to pull location data, maps, and geographic details.
  - o **Financial APIs**: Provide access to real-time stock prices, financial statements, and other economic data.
- **Applications of APIs**:
  - o **Social Media Analytics**: Gathering social media posts, comments, and engagement metrics for analysis.
  - o **Weather Data**: Collecting weather information from sources like **OpenWeatherMap API** to forecast and analyze environmental conditions.
  - o **Real-Time Data Integration**: Pulling live data, such as traffic information, sports scores, or currency exchange rates, for use in applications.
- **Challenges**: Using APIs often comes with rate limits and usage restrictions, and relying on external APIs may introduce data availability and consistency issues.

## *IoT Devices and Real-Time Data Collection*

### 1. IoT (Internet of Things): A Network of Devices Generating Data

IoT refers to the growing network of connected devices that generate and exchange data. These devices can range from smart home appliances like thermostats and refrigerators to industrial machines, vehicles, and wearable devices. The data generated by IoT devices is often streamed in real time, making it an essential component of big data analytics.

- **How IoT Devices Collect Data**:
  - o IoT devices are embedded with sensors that continuously monitor and collect data, which is transmitted to centralized servers or cloud platforms.
  - o Real-time data collected by IoT devices is often analyzed using **streaming analytics** tools such as **Apache Kafka, Apache Flink**, or **AWS Kinesis**.
- **Applications of IoT Data**:
  - o **Smart Homes**: IoT devices such as **smart thermostats** (e.g., Nest) collect data on temperature, humidity, and occupancy to optimize energy usage and enhance convenience.
  - o **Smart Cities**: IoT sensors embedded in street lights, traffic signals, and waste bins collect data to improve

urban planning, traffic management, and public services.

- o **Healthcare**: Wearable devices, such as fitness trackers and smartwatches, monitor patient health metrics (e.g., heart rate, sleep patterns) and send this data to healthcare providers for analysis and personalized care.

- **Challenges**: Managing the large amounts of data generated by IoT devices requires scalable storage solutions and efficient real-time processing frameworks. Data privacy and security are also critical concerns, especially when dealing with sensitive health or personal information.

## 2. Real-Time Data Collection: The Need for Instant Analysis

The ability to collect and analyze data in real time is a powerful advantage in many industries. Real-time data collection enables businesses to make immediate decisions based on up-to-date information.

- **Real-Time Use Cases**:
  - o **Fraud Detection**: Financial institutions can analyze transaction data as it is being made to detect unusual behavior and prevent fraud.
  - o **Autonomous Vehicles**: Self-driving cars collect and analyze data from sensors in real time to make split-second driving decisions.

○ **Social Media Sentiment Analysis**: Analyzing social media posts as they are published can provide insights into public sentiment on various topics.

- **Challenges**: Real-time data processing requires high-performance computing and low-latency systems to ensure that decisions can be made quickly. It also involves handling continuous streams of data, which can be difficult to manage at scale.

---

### *Real-World Example: Data Collection in Smart Cities*

Smart cities use big data to improve the quality of life for residents, enhance sustainability, and optimize urban services. By collecting data from a wide range of **IoT devices**, **sensors**, and **social media**, smart cities can make data-driven decisions to manage traffic, reduce energy consumption, and improve public safety.

#### How Data Collection Works in Smart Cities

- **Traffic Management**: IoT sensors and cameras embedded in roads, intersections, and vehicles collect real-time data on traffic flow, accidents, and congestion. This data is analyzed to adjust traffic light patterns, manage road maintenance schedules, and inform commuters of traffic conditions.

- **Energy Efficiency**: Smart meters in homes and businesses collect data on energy consumption, helping utilities optimize energy distribution and promote energy-saving initiatives. Cities can also manage street lighting by adjusting brightness based on real-time conditions, saving energy during off-peak hours.

- **Waste Management**: Smart trash bins equipped with sensors track waste levels, optimizing collection routes and schedules. This data helps cities minimize waste-related traffic and optimize disposal processes.
- **Public Safety**: IoT devices, cameras, and sensors are used for surveillance, monitoring environmental conditions, and enhancing emergency response times. For example, in the event of a natural disaster, real-time data can help coordinate rescue efforts.

## Challenges in Smart City Data Collection

- **Data Integration**: Collecting data from various sources (sensors, cameras, social media) can be challenging due to differences in data formats and systems. Ensuring seamless integration and real-time analysis is critical for effective decision-making.
- **Privacy and Security**: As smart cities gather data on residents, it is crucial to protect personal information and ensure that data collection does not infringe on privacy rights.

In this chapter, we explored how big data is collected from a wide variety of sources, including **sensors**, **social media**, **web scraping**, **APIs**, and **IoT devices**. Each of these methods offers distinct advantages and challenges in the context of big data, depending on the type of data being collected and the application. Real-time data collection, particularly through IoT devices, has emerged as a key component of modern data-driven solutions.

The **real-world example** of **smart cities** highlighted how data collection and analysis are being used to optimize urban services, improve sustainability, and enhance quality of life for residents. As big data continues to expand, effective data collection methods will be essential in ensuring that businesses, governments, and organizations can harness its power for positive change.

In the next chapter, we will explore **data storage solutions**, focusing on the differences between **data lakes** and **data warehouses**, and how they support big data processing and analysis.

# Chapter 5: Data Storage and Management

Data storage and management are fundamental components of the **big data ecosystem**. As data volumes continue to grow exponentially, organizations need robust, scalable, and efficient ways to store, manage, and access data. This chapter will explore key data storage technologies, including **NoSQL databases**, the **Hadoop Distributed File System (HDFS)**, and **cloud storage solutions**. We will also examine a **real-world example** of **data storage** in the **e-commerce** industry, focusing on how big data is used to manage **customer data** effectively.

---

## *NoSQL Databases: MongoDB, Cassandra, and More*

**NoSQL databases** have become increasingly popular for handling big data due to their ability to store and manage large volumes of unstructured and semi-structured data. Unlike traditional relational databases that store data in tables with predefined schemas, NoSQL databases offer greater flexibility in how data is stored and accessed.

### 1. What is NoSQL?

NoSQL stands for "Not Only SQL," and it refers to a broad category of databases that are designed to handle unstructured data, provide scalability, and allow for flexible data models. NoSQL databases are well-suited for big data applications that require horizontal scaling and high availability.

## 2. Types of NoSQL Databases

There are four main types of NoSQL databases:

- **Document Stores**: These databases store data in documents, typically in JSON or BSON format. Each document can contain different fields, making document stores highly flexible. Examples include:
  - **MongoDB**: One of the most widely used document stores, MongoDB allows for easy scaling and flexible schema design. It is popular for web applications, content management systems, and other big data use cases.
  - **CouchDB**: Another document-oriented database, CouchDB uses a schema-free design and supports both HTTP API access and RESTful queries.
- **Key-Value Stores**: These databases store data as key-value pairs, where each key is associated with a value. Key-value stores are ideal for high-performance scenarios where quick lookups are needed. Examples include:
  - **Redis**: An in-memory key-value store used for caching, session management, and real-time data processing.

- o **Riak**: A distributed key-value store that provides high availability and fault tolerance.
- **Column Family Stores**: These databases store data in columns rather than rows, making them ideal for read-heavy workloads and analytical applications. Examples include:
  - o **Cassandra**: An open-source, distributed column family store that can handle massive amounts of data across many servers without a single point of failure. It is often used for real-time analytics and log data collection.
  - o **HBase**: A column-oriented database that is part of the Hadoop ecosystem, designed to store large amounts of sparse data.
- **Graph Databases**: These databases are designed to handle complex relationships between data entities, making them ideal for use cases involving social networks, fraud detection, and recommendation engines. Examples include:
  - o **Neo4j**: A widely used graph database that stores data in graph structures, with nodes representing entities and edges representing relationships.

## 3. Advantages of NoSQL Databases

- **Scalability**: NoSQL databases can scale horizontally, meaning they can handle growing data loads by adding more machines to the network.

- **Flexibility**: NoSQL databases do not require a predefined schema, making them ideal for applications where the data structure may change over time.
- **Performance**: NoSQL databases are optimized for high-speed read and write operations, making them ideal for real-time applications.

## 4. Use Cases for NoSQL

- **E-Commerce**: Storing product catalogs, user preferences, and transaction data.
- **Social Media**: Handling user-generated content, likes, shares, and comments.
- **IoT**: Storing data generated by connected devices and sensors.

## *Hadoop Distributed File System (HDFS)*

**HDFS** is a distributed storage system that allows large datasets to be stored across multiple machines, with redundancy built in for fault tolerance. It is a core component of the **Apache Hadoop** ecosystem and is designed to store vast amounts of data in a way that is scalable, fault-tolerant, and highly available.

## 1. How HDFS Works

HDFS divides large files into smaller **blocks** (typically 128MB or 256MB) and distributes them across a cluster of machines. Each block is replicated multiple times to ensure fault tolerance, meaning that if one machine fails, the data is still available from another machine that has a copy of the block.

- **Block Storage**: HDFS stores files as large blocks, which are distributed across multiple nodes in the cluster. Each block is replicated for redundancy.
- **Master-Slave Architecture**: HDFS follows a master-slave architecture where the **NameNode** is the master server that manages metadata and the **DataNodes** are slave servers that store actual data blocks.

## 2. Advantages of HDFS

- **Fault Tolerance**: With data replication, HDFS ensures that even if some nodes fail, the data remains available without any loss.
- **Scalability**: HDFS is designed to scale horizontally, meaning it can store petabytes of data across many machines without performance degradation.
- **Cost-Effective**: HDFS is often used in conjunction with commodity hardware, making it an affordable solution for big data storage.

## 3. Use Cases for HDFS

- **Data Lakes**: HDFS is often used as the backbone of a data lake, where raw and unprocessed data is stored before being processed by big data tools.
- **Log Analysis**: HDFS is ideal for storing large volumes of log data generated by websites, applications, and systems.

## *Cloud Storage Solutions for Big Data*

Cloud storage solutions are transforming the way organizations manage and store big data. By using cloud platforms, businesses can store vast amounts of data without investing in physical hardware or infrastructure. Cloud storage also provides the scalability, flexibility, and cost-effectiveness needed to handle big data.

### 1. Key Cloud Storage Providers

- **Amazon Web Services (AWS)**: AWS offers services like **Amazon S3 (Simple Storage Service)** for scalable object storage, **Amazon EFS (Elastic File System)** for file storage, and **Amazon Glacier** for long-term data archiving.
- **Google Cloud Platform (GCP)**: Google Cloud offers **Cloud Storage**, which is a highly scalable object storage service, as well as **BigQuery** for data analytics.
- **Microsoft Azure**: Azure provides cloud storage services like **Azure Blob Storage** and **Azure Data Lake Storage**, which are designed for big data workloads.

## 2. Advantages of Cloud Storage

- **Scalability**: Cloud storage solutions can automatically scale to accommodate growing data volumes, ensuring that businesses can store and process large datasets without worrying about infrastructure limitations.
- **Accessibility**: Cloud storage allows for easy access to data from anywhere in the world, which is essential for global businesses or remote teams.
- **Cost-Efficiency**: Many cloud storage providers offer pay-as-you-go models, allowing businesses to pay only for the storage they actually use, making it a cost-effective solution.

## 3. Use Cases for Cloud Storage

- **Backup and Disaster Recovery**: Cloud storage is often used for data backup and disaster recovery solutions, ensuring that data is safe in case of hardware failure.
- **Data Lakes**: Cloud providers offer **data lake** services where businesses can store large volumes of raw data in a cost-effective and scalable way.
- **Real-Time Analytics**: Cloud platforms enable businesses to process and analyze big data in real-time, making it ideal for applications such as fraud detection, IoT, and personalized recommendations.

### *Real-World Example: Data Storage in E-Commerce (Customer Data Management)*

One of the most prominent applications of big data storage solutions is in the **e-commerce** industry, where managing and analyzing customer data is crucial for providing personalized shopping experiences, improving sales, and optimizing inventory.

#### How Data Storage Works in E-Commerce

- **Customer Profiles**: E-commerce platforms store large amounts of customer data, including **purchase history**, **preferences**, **browsing behavior**, and **location data**. This data is often stored in **NoSQL databases** like **MongoDB** or **Cassandra**, as it is unstructured and constantly evolving.
- **Product Data**: Data about products, including **inventory levels**, **prices**, and **reviews**, is stored in **relational databases** or **NoSQL databases** depending on the volume and structure of the data.
- **Transactional Data**: Every transaction made on the e-commerce platform, including payment information, order history, and shipping details, is stored in databases for tracking and analysis.

#### Big Data in E-Commerce Applications

- **Personalized Recommendations**: By analyzing customer purchase history and behavior, e-commerce platforms can provide **personalized product recommendations**. This data is typically stored in **data lakes** and processed using tools like **Apache Spark** for real-time recommendation algorithms.

- **Customer Segmentation**: E-commerce companies use big data to segment their customers based on factors such as purchasing patterns, demographics, and online behavior. This allows for targeted marketing campaigns and personalized promotions.

- **Supply Chain Optimization**: Big data analytics helps e-commerce companies optimize their supply chains by analyzing sales data, customer demand, and inventory levels. This data can be stored in cloud storage and processed using **Hadoop** or **Google BigQuery**.

## Challenges in Data Storage for E-Commerce

- **Data Privacy and Security**: E-commerce platforms must protect sensitive customer information, such as payment details, using encryption and access control mechanisms.

- **Scalability**: As the number of transactions and customer profiles increases, the data storage solution must scale to accommodate growing data volumes.

In this chapter, we explored various **data storage and management** solutions critical to big data. We delved into the features and use cases of **NoSQL databases** like **MongoDB** and **Cassandra**, which are ideal for handling large, unstructured data sets. We also discussed the importance of the **Hadoop Distributed File System (HDFS)** for large-scale data storage and processing, and the benefits of **cloud storage solutions** that provide scalable and cost-effective ways to store and manage big data.

We highlighted a **real-world example** of how **e-commerce** companies manage customer data, use big data analytics for **personalization**, and optimize their operations with data-driven insights. As we move forward, we will dive deeper into the **data processing** and **analytics** frameworks that allow organizations to extract value from their big data and make data-driven decisions.

# Chapter 6: Data Processing Frameworks

Data processing is one of the most critical components of the **big data pipeline**, where raw data is transformed into valuable insights. Due to the sheer volume and complexity of data, traditional data processing tools are often not sufficient. As a result, **distributed computing** frameworks have emerged to handle the massive scale of big data, enabling organizations to process data across multiple machines or clusters. In this chapter, we will introduce the concept of distributed computing, delve into two major **data processing frameworks—Apache Hadoop** with **MapReduce**, and **Apache Spark**—and conclude with a **real-world example** of how Netflix uses big data processing to power its **recommendation engine**.

---

### *Introduction to Distributed Computing*

**Distributed computing** refers to the use of multiple computers, or nodes, to work together on a single task. In the context of big data, distributed computing enables the processing of vast amounts of data that would otherwise be too large for a single machine to handle. By dividing the workload across many machines, distributed systems can process data more efficiently and scale to handle larger datasets.

Why Distributed Computing is Essential for Big Data

- **Scalability**: As data volumes grow, distributed computing allows organizations to scale their infrastructure by adding more nodes to the cluster, rather than relying on more powerful hardware.
- **Fault Tolerance**: Distributed systems are designed to handle node failures. Data is replicated across multiple nodes, ensuring that if one machine fails, the data can still be accessed from another.
- **Parallel Processing**: Distributed computing enables parallel processing, where tasks are split into smaller jobs that can be processed simultaneously, speeding up computation times.

## Key Components of Distributed Computing

- **Nodes**: Individual machines or virtual machines in a distributed system that contribute to processing data.
- **Cluster**: A collection of nodes that work together as part of a distributed system.
- **Master and Worker Nodes**: In many distributed frameworks, the master node coordinates the overall operation, while worker nodes handle specific tasks.

---

### *Apache Hadoop and MapReduce*

**Apache Hadoop** is one of the most popular distributed computing frameworks, designed to process and store large datasets across a distributed cluster of computers. Hadoop was built to scale from a single server to thousands of machines and provides a reliable, fault-tolerant system for data processing.

## 1. What is Apache Hadoop?

Apache Hadoop is an open-source framework that allows organizations to store and process vast amounts of data in a distributed manner. It consists of two core components:

- **Hadoop Distributed File System (HDFS)**: A distributed file system that splits large files into smaller blocks and stores them across multiple machines in the cluster. HDFS is fault-tolerant and ensures data availability by replicating blocks across different nodes.
- **MapReduce**: A programming model and processing engine that enables parallel processing of data across multiple nodes.

## 2. How MapReduce Works

MapReduce is a key component of Hadoop that facilitates the parallel processing of large datasets. The model is divided into two main phases:

- **Map Phase**: The input data is split into smaller chunks (called splits), and the "mapper" function processes each chunk in parallel. The mapper produces a list of intermediate key-value pairs.

- **Reduce Phase**: The output from the map phase is grouped by key, and the "reducer" function processes the grouped data. The reducer combines the values associated with each key to produce the final output.

MapReduce is designed to process large datasets by distributing the computation across many machines, which enables Hadoop to scale for big data.

## 3. Advantages and Challenges of Hadoop

- **Advantages**:
  - **Scalability**: Hadoop can scale horizontally by adding more machines to the cluster.
  - **Fault Tolerance**: Data is replicated across multiple nodes, ensuring that the system can handle failures without data loss.
  - **Cost-Effectiveness**: Hadoop can run on commodity hardware, making it an affordable solution for processing large datasets.
- **Challenges**:
  - **Latency**: MapReduce can be slow, especially for iterative tasks or jobs that require multiple rounds of processing.

o **Complexity**: Writing and debugging MapReduce jobs can be complex and require knowledge of distributed computing concepts.

---

## *Apache Spark: Speed and Scalability*

While Hadoop's MapReduce has been a cornerstone for big data processing, **Apache Spark** has emerged as a faster and more flexible alternative. Spark provides an in-memory processing framework that allows for real-time data analytics and faster computation compared to traditional MapReduce.

### 1. What is Apache Spark?

Apache Spark is an open-source, distributed computing framework designed for fast, in-memory processing of large datasets. Unlike Hadoop's MapReduce, which writes intermediate results to disk between each step, Spark keeps intermediate data in memory, which leads to significant performance improvements, especially for iterative algorithms.

### 2. How Apache Spark Works

- **In-Memory Processing**: Spark processes data in memory (RAM), significantly reducing the time needed to read from and write to disk compared to MapReduce.

- **Resilient Distributed Datasets (RDDs)**: RDDs are the fundamental data structure in Spark. They are immutable collections of data that are distributed across the cluster. RDDs can be processed in parallel across multiple nodes, and transformations or actions can be applied to them.

- **Transformations and Actions**: In Spark, operations on RDDs are categorized as transformations (e.g., map(), filter()) and actions (e.g., count(), collect()). Transformations are lazily evaluated, meaning they are not computed until an action is triggered.

## 3. Advantages of Apache Spark

- **Speed**: Spark's in-memory processing allows it to be much faster than Hadoop MapReduce, especially for iterative tasks.

- **Ease of Use**: Spark supports high-level APIs in languages like Python, Java, and Scala, making it more accessible than Hadoop's lower-level MapReduce programming model.

- **Real-Time Data Processing**: Spark includes **Spark Streaming**, which enables the processing of real-time data, making it suitable for applications like fraud detection, monitoring, and recommendations.

## 4. Use Cases for Apache Spark

- **Real-Time Analytics**: Spark can process real-time data, making it ideal for applications that require instant insights, such as financial fraud detection or online activity monitoring.

- **Machine Learning**: Spark includes **MLlib**, a scalable machine learning library that allows users to build and train models on large datasets.

- **Data Integration and ETL**: Spark is commonly used for extracting, transforming, and loading (ETL) large datasets from multiple sources.

## 5. Apache Spark vs. Hadoop

While both Spark and Hadoop are used for distributed data processing, the main difference lies in performance and flexibility:

- **Speed**: Spark is faster than Hadoop MapReduce because it processes data in memory rather than writing intermediate results to disk.

- **Ease of Use**: Spark has a simpler API and supports high-level programming languages like Python, making it easier to develop applications.

- **Real-Time Processing**: Spark supports real-time processing through **Spark Streaming**, while Hadoop is generally suited for batch processing.

---

*Real-World Example: Data Processing for Movie Streaming (Netflix's Recommendation Engine)*

One of the most prominent examples of big data processing in action is **Netflix's recommendation engine**, which relies heavily on distributed computing frameworks like **Apache Spark** for data processing.

## How Netflix Uses Big Data Processing

Netflix uses big data to personalize content recommendations for its users. The recommendation engine analyzes vast amounts of data, including:

- **Viewing history**: What movies and shows a user has watched.
- **Ratings**: How users rate the content they watch.
- **Search behavior**: What users search for within the platform.
- **Demographics**: Age, location, and preferences of users.

## 1. Data Collection and Storage

Netflix collects data from its users in real time, including viewing data, search queries, and social media interactions. This data is stored in **data lakes** or **distributed storage systems**.

## 2. Data Processing with Apache Spark

Once collected, this data is processed using **Apache Spark**. Spark performs a variety of transformations on the data, such as:

- **Collaborative Filtering**: Spark uses collaborative filtering algorithms to identify patterns in user behavior and recommend content that is similar to what other users with similar preferences have watched.

- **Content-Based Filtering**: Spark analyzes content attributes (e.g., genre, actors, directors) to recommend movies or shows that are similar to what a user has watched previously.

### 3. Real-Time Recommendations

Spark's **real-time data processing** capabilities enable Netflix to make immediate recommendations based on a user's latest viewing activity. This allows the platform to offer personalized suggestions as users browse or continue watching.

### 4. Machine Learning

Netflix employs machine learning models to improve the accuracy of its recommendations. Spark's **MLlib** library is used to train machine learning models on large-scale datasets, enabling Netflix to predict which movies or shows a user is most likely to enjoy.

### 5. A/B Testing

Netflix also uses A/B testing to experiment with different recommendation algorithms. By analyzing the performance of different models on subsets of users, Netflix can determine which model provides the best user experience.

### Impact

- **Personalization**: Big data processing allows Netflix to deliver highly personalized recommendations to users, keeping them engaged and reducing churn.

- **Customer Satisfaction**: By providing users with relevant content suggestions, Netflix enhances customer satisfaction and loyalty.

---

In this chapter, we introduced the concept of **distributed computing** and how it underpins the success of big data processing frameworks. We explored **Apache Hadoop** with **MapReduce** and **Apache Spark**, highlighting their strengths, use cases, and differences. We also examined a **real-world example** of how Netflix uses big data processing to power its **recommendation engine**, improving the user experience and driving customer retention.

The ability to process large datasets quickly and efficiently is crucial in today's data-driven world. In the following chapters, we will explore additional tools and frameworks that help organizations process, analyze, and visualize big data for actionable insights.

# Chapter 7: Data Cleaning and Preparation

Before diving into advanced analysis or building models, it is crucial to ensure that the data is clean, consistent, and well-structured. **Data cleaning and preparation** are often the most time-consuming and important steps in the data science workflow. This chapter will cover the importance of data cleaning, common techniques for data preprocessing and transformation, how to handle missing or inconsistent data, and conclude with a **real-world example** of **data cleaning** in **financial analysis**.

---

### *The Importance of Data Cleaning*

In any data science or machine learning project, **data cleaning** is a crucial step that directly affects the quality of the insights and the accuracy of the models. Raw data is often messy, incomplete, or inconsistent, and without proper cleaning, the analysis could lead to misleading s. Data cleaning helps improve the quality of the data, ensuring that it is accurate, complete, and in a format suitable for analysis.

Why Data Cleaning Matters

- **Accuracy**: Clean data ensures that the analysis is based on accurate information, preventing errors in modeling or decision-making.
- **Consistency**: Inconsistent data, such as different formats for the same information (e.g., "USA" vs. "United States"), can lead to misinterpretations. Cleaning ensures that similar values are represented consistently.
- **Efficiency**: Clean data accelerates the process of building models and generating insights, as it is easier to work with structured and well-organized data.
- **Improved Results**: Well-prepared data results in more accurate and reliable predictions, leading to better business outcomes.

Without proper data cleaning, analyses can be biased, incomplete, or even wrong, which can significantly impact decision-making processes. In the next section, we will look at the different **data preprocessing and transformation** techniques that are commonly used to prepare data for analysis.

---

## *Techniques for Data Preprocessing and Transformation*

**Data preprocessing** refers to the steps taken to transform raw data into a format suitable for analysis. It typically involves cleaning, transforming, and normalizing data to make it more usable. Below are some of the most common techniques used in data preprocessing:

## 1. Normalization and Standardization

- **Normalization** refers to scaling features to a specific range, typically [0, 1]. This is particularly useful when different features in a dataset have different units or ranges. For example, if one feature is income (ranging from $10,000 to $100,000) and another feature is age (ranging from 20 to 70), normalizing both features ensures that they are on the same scale.

- **Standardization** involves rescaling features so that they have a **mean of 0** and a **standard deviation of 1**. This is useful when the data has varying units or when the model requires normally distributed data.

  Common Python libraries for normalization and standardization:

  o **scikit-learn**: StandardScaler, MinMaxScaler

## 2. Encoding Categorical Variables

Data preprocessing also involves converting **categorical variables** (variables that take on discrete values, such as "male" and "female") into a numerical format that machine learning algorithms can interpret.

- **One-Hot Encoding**: One-hot encoding converts categorical variables into binary (0 or 1) columns, with each column representing one category.

- **Label Encoding**: Label encoding assigns each category a unique number, but this can be problematic for algorithms that may interpret the encoded values as ordinal (i.e., with inherent order).

Common tools for encoding categorical variables:

- **Pandas**: get_dummies(), factorize()
- **scikit-learn**: OneHotEncoder, LabelEncoder

## 3. Feature Engineering

Feature engineering is the process of creating new features or modifying existing ones to improve the performance of a machine learning model. This may include:

- **Aggregating data**: For example, creating a new feature representing the average monthly spending from daily transaction data.

- **Extracting new information**: For instance, extracting the year or month from a timestamp to create new features like "year" or "month."

## 4. Data Transformation

- **Log Transformation**: For data that is skewed or has outliers, a log transformation can help to reduce skewness and stabilize variance.
- **Box-Cox Transformation**: This transformation is used to stabilize variance and make data more normally distributed.

---

## *Dealing with Missing and Inconsistent Data*

One of the most common challenges in data preparation is dealing with **missing** or **inconsistent** data. Incomplete or incorrect data can lead to incorrect analysis or biased results. Here are some strategies to handle missing or inconsistent data:

### 1. Handling Missing Data

- **Removal**: The simplest approach is to remove rows or columns with missing data. This may be appropriate if the missing data is not critical or if there are only a small number of missing values.
- **Imputation**: If the missing values represent a significant portion of the data, imputation techniques can be used to fill in the gaps:
  - **Mean/Median Imputation**: Replacing missing values with the mean or median value of the column.

- ○ **Predictive Imputation**: Using machine learning models to predict missing values based on other features.
- ○ **K-Nearest Neighbors Imputation**: Imputing missing values based on the values of similar rows.
- **Forward/Backward Filling**: In time series data, missing values can often be filled by using the previous (or next) value in the sequence.

## 2. Handling Inconsistent Data

- **Duplicate Data**: Duplicates often arise during data collection, and they can skew results. Removing duplicates ensures that each observation is unique.

  Common techniques:

  - ○ **Pandas**: drop_duplicates()
- **Outliers**: Outliers are extreme values that may be the result of errors or unusual but valid cases. Handling outliers can involve:
  - ○ Removing them.
  - ○ Transforming them (e.g., using a log transformation).
  - ○ Capping or winsorizing the data (limiting the maximum and minimum values).
- **Inconsistent Formats**: Data can be inconsistent in terms of formats, such as dates recorded in different formats ("2021-

05-01" vs. "01/05/2021"). Standardizing data formats is crucial for consistency.

Common tools:

o **Pandas**: to_datetime() for standardizing dates.

---

## Real-World Example: Data Cleaning in Financial Analysis

In the financial industry, data cleaning is critical for accurate analysis and decision-making. Financial institutions often deal with large volumes of transactional data, stock market data, customer information, and more, all of which need to be cleaned and prepared for analysis.

### 1. Handling Missing Data in Financial Transactions

Financial institutions often face missing data in transactional records, such as missing timestamps or missing transaction amounts. To handle this:

- **Imputation** might be used for missing transaction amounts based on the average transaction size in the same category (e.g., "grocery store purchases").
- **Forward filling** might be used for missing timestamps, ensuring that the time gaps between transactions are consistent.

## 2. Identifying and Removing Duplicate Transactions

Duplicate transactions can occur when multiple records are created for the same financial event, either due to system errors or human input mistakes. These duplicates must be identified and removed to ensure accurate financial reporting.

## 3. Dealing with Inconsistent Data Formats

In a financial dataset, dates may be recorded in various formats, such as **YYYY-MM-DD** or **MM/DD/YYYY**. For consistency, all dates would be standardized to a single format using tools like **Pandas' to_datetime()** function.

## 4. Correcting Data Entry Errors

Human errors often introduce inconsistencies in financial data, such as incorrect customer names or transaction amounts. These errors need to be flagged and corrected to ensure the integrity of the data. This can be done by validating entries against known datasets (e.g., comparing customer names with a reference list of customers) or using imputation strategies to fill in missing values.

## 5. Handling Outliers in Financial Data

In financial datasets, outliers could represent fraud, system errors, or rare but valid occurrences. For example, an unusually large transaction may be an outlier, but it could also be a legitimate purchase. To handle outliers:

- **Visualizations** like box plots or histograms can help identify extreme values.

- **Domain knowledge** can be used to distinguish between valid outliers and errors (e.g., a $10,000 transaction in a small account might be an error, but in a larger account, it could be legitimate).

## 6. Data Transformation for Financial Analysis

In financial analysis, log transformations or percentage changes might be used to transform highly skewed data (e.g., transaction amounts). This helps normalize the data for modeling and ensures that extreme values don't disproportionately impact the results.

---

In this chapter, we discussed the importance of **data cleaning and preparation**, emphasizing that clean data is essential for accurate analysis and model building. We explored key data preprocessing techniques, including **normalization**, **categorical encoding**, **feature engineering**, and **data transformation**. We also covered methods for handling **missing and inconsistent data**, such as imputation, removal, and formatting corrections.

Finally, we provided a **real-world example** from the **financial industry**, demonstrating how data cleaning is applied to transactional and financial data to ensure accuracy, consistency, and reliability in analysis.

As we move forward, the next step will involve exploring **data transformation** in greater detail and looking at how data can be used effectively for building machine learning models and driving business decisions.

# Chapter 8: Exploring Data with SQL and NoSQL

As big data continues to grow, organizations must be equipped with the right tools to query, analyze, and extract insights from massive datasets. Traditional **SQL** databases and modern **NoSQL** databases each have their strengths and are used in different scenarios based on the nature of the data and the requirements of the application. In this chapter, we will explore the differences between SQL and NoSQL databases, focusing on their capabilities for querying big data. We will also examine two popular NoSQL databases, **MongoDB** and **Cassandra**, and conclude with a **real-world example** of using **SQL** for **sales analytics**.

---

### *Querying Big Data with SQL*

**SQL (Structured Query Language)** has been the foundation of database management for decades. Relational databases use SQL to store and manage structured data in tables with rows and columns, making SQL a powerful tool for querying data.

### 1. SQL: A Query Language for Structured Data

SQL is used to interact with relational databases, and it allows users to:

- **Create** and **manage** databases and tables.

- **Insert**, **update**, and **delete** records.
- **Select** data using complex queries with filtering, sorting, and aggregation.

SQL is highly effective for querying structured data that fits well within a **relational schema**. It is ideal for applications where data relationships are well-defined, such as inventory management, financial reporting, or customer relationship management (CRM).

## 2. Key SQL Operations

- **SELECT**: The most common SQL operation, used to retrieve data from tables.

sql

```
SELECT column1, column2 FROM table_name WHERE condition;
```

- **JOIN**: Combines data from two or more tables based on a related column.

sql

```
SELECT orders.order_id, customers.customer_name
FROM orders
JOIN customers ON orders.customer_id = customers.customer_id;
```

- **GROUP BY**: Aggregates data based on a specified column, useful for summarizing large datasets.

sql

```
SELECT product_name, SUM(sales) FROM sales_data GROUP BY
product_name;
```

- **ORDER BY**: Sorts the result set by one or more columns.

sql

```
SELECT product_name, sales FROM sales_data ORDER BY sales
DESC;
```

## 3. SQL for Big Data

Although SQL is traditionally associated with relational databases, modern **SQL-on-Hadoop** solutions allow SQL queries to be executed on large datasets stored in distributed environments, such as Hadoop and cloud-based systems. Tools like **Apache Hive**, **Apache Impala**, and **Google BigQuery** extend the power of SQL to big data, enabling users to run SQL-like queries on massive datasets.

---

## *NoSQL Databases: What Makes Them Different?*

While SQL databases are a good fit for structured data, **NoSQL** databases have emerged to handle the demands of big data, particularly when dealing with unstructured or semi-structured data. NoSQL databases differ from SQL databases in several key areas:

## 1. What is NoSQL?

NoSQL stands for "Not Only SQL" and refers to a broad class of databases that do not rely on the relational model. NoSQL databases are designed to handle large volumes of data with flexible schemas, scalability, and high availability.

## 2. Key Differences Between SQL and NoSQL

| Aspect | SQL | NoSQL |
|---|---|---|
| Data Model | Relational (tables, rows, columns) | Non-relational (key-value, document, column-family, graph) |
| Schema | Fixed schema (predefined structure) | Flexible schema (no predefined structure) |
| Scalability | Vertical scaling (increasing hardware) | Horizontal scaling (adding more nodes) |
| Transactions | Strong ACID (Atomicity, Consistency, Isolation, Durability) | Eventual consistency (sometimes eventual consistency) |
| Query Language | SQL (Structured Query Language) | No standard query language (depends on the database type) |

## 3. When to Use NoSQL

NoSQL databases are ideal when:

- Data is unstructured or semi-structured, such as JSON, XML, or key-value pairs.
- The schema is flexible, and the data model may evolve over time.
- Horizontal scaling is required to handle growing data loads.
- Real-time data processing or analytics is needed, as NoSQL databases can offer lower latency than traditional relational databases.

---

### *MongoDB and Cassandra for Big Data*

Two of the most popular NoSQL databases for big data applications are **MongoDB** and **Cassandra**. These databases are designed to handle massive amounts of data with flexibility, scalability, and performance.

## 1. MongoDB

**MongoDB** is a document-oriented NoSQL database that stores data in flexible, JSON-like documents called **BSON** (Binary JSON). This format allows for a nested, hierarchical structure, making MongoDB well-suited for unstructured or semi-structured data.

- **Key Features**:

- Flexible Schema: MongoDB allows for a dynamic schema, meaning that different documents in the same collection can have different fields.
- Horizontal Scaling: MongoDB supports **sharding**, a technique for distributing data across multiple servers to handle large datasets.
- Rich Query Language: MongoDB provides a rich query language that allows for complex queries, including aggregations and full-text search.

- Use Cases:
  - Content Management Systems: Storing and managing articles, images, and metadata.
  - Real-Time Analytics: Storing and processing real-time user activity or sensor data.
  - E-commerce: Managing product catalogs, customer data, and transactions.

## 2. Cassandra

**Apache Cassandra** is a distributed, highly scalable NoSQL database designed to handle massive amounts of data across many commodity servers. It is a **column-family store**, which means it organizes data into columns rather than rows, optimizing it for read-heavy operations.

- **Key Features**:

- o **Distributed Architecture**: Cassandra is built to run on clusters of machines, ensuring high availability and fault tolerance.

- o **Write Optimized**: Cassandra is optimized for write-heavy workloads, making it ideal for applications that require fast data ingestion.

- o **Eventual Consistency**: Cassandra uses an **eventual consistency** model, meaning that it sacrifices immediate consistency for high availability and performance.

- **Use Cases**:

  - o **IoT**: Handling large volumes of data generated by connected devices.

  - o **Log Data Analysis**: Storing logs from web servers, applications, and networks for analysis.

  - o **Real-Time Analytics**: Processing large-scale data for real-time business intelligence.

---

### Real-World Example: Using SQL for Sales Analytics

A common application of SQL in big data is **sales analytics**, where organizations need to analyze large volumes of sales data to make data-driven decisions. In this example, we will explore how SQL can be used to analyze sales data in a relational database.

Sales Data Example

Let's say an e-commerce company wants to analyze sales data stored in a relational database to understand:

- **Total sales by region**.
- **Sales growth** over time.
- **Top-selling products**.

The sales data is stored in the following tables:

- **Products**: Contains product information, including product ID, name, and category.
- **Sales**: Contains sales transaction data, including transaction ID, product ID, quantity, sale date, and sales amount.
- **Customers**: Contains customer information, including customer ID, name, and location.

## SQL Query for Total Sales by Region

sql

```
SELECT customers.region, SUM(sales.sales_amount) AS total_sales
FROM sales
JOIN customers ON sales.customer_id = customers.customer_id
GROUP BY customers.region;
```

This query joins the **Sales** and **Customers** tables and calculates the total sales for each region by grouping the data by the region and summing the sales amount.

## SQL Query for Sales Growth Over Time

sql

```
SELECT YEAR(sales.sale_date) AS year, SUM(sales.sales_amount) AS
total_sales
FROM sales
GROUP BY YEAR(sales.sale_date)
ORDER BY year;
```

This query groups the sales data by year, sums the sales amount, and orders the results by year to analyze the growth in sales over time.

## SQL Query for Top-Selling Products

sql

```
SELECT products.product_name, SUM(sales.quantity) AS total_units_sold
FROM sales
JOIN products ON sales.product_id = products.product_id
GROUP BY products.product_name
ORDER BY total_units_sold DESC
LIMIT 10;
```

This query calculates the total quantity of each product sold, groups the data by product name, and orders the results to show the top-selling products.

## Outcome

Using SQL to analyze sales data provides valuable insights into product performance, regional sales patterns, and overall business growth. By querying relational databases, businesses can gain a deeper understanding of their sales data and make informed decisions on inventory, marketing, and pricing strategies.

In this chapter, we explored the fundamentals of querying big data with **SQL** and **NoSQL** databases. We discussed the key differences between SQL and NoSQL, highlighting when each type of database is best suited for different types of data and use cases. We also examined **MongoDB** and **Cassandra**, two widely used NoSQL databases, and how they are optimized for handling big data.

Finally, we looked at a **real-world example** of using **SQL** for **sales analytics**, demonstrating how SQL queries can be used to extract meaningful insights from large datasets in e-commerce.

As we continue, we will dive deeper into **advanced data analysis techniques** and explore how organizations can leverage big data for business intelligence, machine learning, and decision-making.

# Chapter 9: Data Visualization

In the era of big data, **data visualization** has become an indispensable tool for understanding and interpreting large datasets. While raw data can be difficult to comprehend, visualizing it in charts, graphs, and other visual formats makes it easier to spot patterns, trends, and outliers. In this chapter, we will explore **best practices** for visualizing big data, review some popular **data visualization tools** like **Tableau**, **Power BI**, and **D3.js**, and discuss the creation of **interactive dashboards** for delivering insights. We will also examine a **real-world example** of **data visualization** in the context of **marketing campaigns**.

---

### *Visualizing Big Data: Best Practices*

When visualizing big data, the goal is to present complex information in a simple, clear, and actionable way. To achieve this, it's essential to follow best practices for data visualization, ensuring that the insights are easy to understand and interpret.

### 1. Understand Your Audience

- **Tailor the Visualization**: Different stakeholders may have varying levels of expertise and interest in the data. For example, executives might prefer high-level insights, while data analysts might need detailed, granular views.

- **Simplicity is Key**: The complexity of big data doesn't have to translate into complex visuals. Strive for clarity and simplicity, using straightforward charts and graphs that make insights easy to grasp.

## 2. Choose the Right Type of Visualization

Different types of data require different types of visualizations. Selecting the appropriate chart or graph depends on the data you are presenting and the story you want to tell.

- **Line Charts**: Ideal for showing trends over time (e.g., sales data over several months).
- **Bar Charts**: Useful for comparing quantities across categories (e.g., sales by product type).
- **Pie Charts**: Best for showing proportions or percentages of a whole (e.g., market share of different brands).
- **Scatter Plots**: Used to show the relationship between two continuous variables (e.g., sales vs. advertising spend).
- **Heatmaps**: Excellent for visualizing data density or intensity (e.g., customer interactions on a website).

## 3. Focus on Key Insights

- **Avoid Overcomplication**: With big data, it's easy to overwhelm your audience with too many details. Focus on the key insights that are most relevant to your audience's objectives.

- **Use Color Wisely**: Colors can help emphasize important points, but they can also confuse or mislead if overused. Stick to a consistent color scheme, using colors to distinguish categories or highlight critical data points.

## 4. Make Data Interactive

When dealing with big data, providing interactivity in your visualizations can help users explore the data in more depth. Interactive features like filters, drill-downs, and zooming allow users to focus on the data most relevant to them.

---

### Tools for Data Visualization: Tableau, Power BI, D3.js

The right tool for data visualization depends on the nature of the data, the level of interactivity required, and the user's technical expertise. Below, we explore three popular tools for creating compelling data visualizations: **Tableau**, **Power BI**, and **D3.js**.

## 1. Tableau

**Tableau** is one of the most widely used data visualization tools, known for its powerful capabilities, ease of use, and flexibility. Tableau is particularly popular for creating interactive dashboards and visualizations without the need for coding.

- **Key Features**:

- o **Drag-and-Drop Interface**: Tableau allows users to easily drag and drop fields to create visualizations without needing programming skills.
- o **Integration**: Tableau can connect to various data sources, including databases, cloud services, and big data platforms like Hadoop.
- o **Real-Time Data Updates**: It supports live connections to data sources, allowing for real-time data visualizations.
- o **Advanced Analytics**: Tableau also offers built-in statistical functions and predictive analytics.
- **Use Cases**:
  - o Business intelligence dashboards.
  - o Data exploration and reporting for decision-makers.
  - o Real-time monitoring and performance tracking.

## 2. Power BI

**Power BI**, developed by Microsoft, is a widely used business analytics tool for creating visual reports and dashboards. Like Tableau, Power BI provides a user-friendly interface and is integrated with other Microsoft tools, making it an excellent choice for businesses using Microsoft products.

- **Key Features**:

- o **Excel Integration**: Power BI integrates seamlessly with Microsoft Excel, allowing users to import and visualize data from spreadsheets.

- o **Cloud and On-Premises**: Power BI offers cloud-based solutions as well as on-premises versions for secure data handling.

- o **Custom Visuals**: Power BI supports the use of custom visualizations, including third-party visuals.

- o **Natural Language Query**: Power BI allows users to query data using natural language (e.g., "What is the total sales for this region?").

- **Use Cases**:
  - o Executive dashboards for decision-makers.
  - o Sales and financial reporting.
  - o Operational monitoring and performance tracking.

## 3. D3.js

**D3.js** (Data-Driven Documents) is a powerful JavaScript library for creating complex, interactive data visualizations on the web. Unlike Tableau and Power BI, which offer drag-and-drop interfaces, D3.js provides more flexibility but requires a solid understanding of JavaScript and web development.

- **Key Features**:

- **Customizable Visualizations**: D3.js allows for complete control over how data is visualized, from simple charts to advanced interactive graphics.
- **Web-Based**: D3.js works directly in web browsers, making it ideal for web-based dashboards and visualizations.
- **Dynamic Data**: D3.js allows users to build dynamic visualizations that change based on real-time data.

- **Use Cases**:
    - Custom web-based visualizations for complex data.
    - Interactive data applications and dashboards for websites.
    - Scientific data visualizations and research publications.

---

## *Interactive Dashboards for Big Data Insights*

Interactive dashboards provide a powerful way to present big data insights in a dynamic and engaging format. By incorporating interactivity, users can explore data at their own pace and uncover insights that are most relevant to them.

### 1. Features of Interactive Dashboards

- **Filters**: Allow users to select subsets of data based on categories or time periods, enabling them to drill down into specific details.

- **Hover-over Tooltips**: Provide additional information when a user hovers over a data point, giving context without cluttering the visualization.

- **Dynamic Sorting**: Let users reorder data, such as sorting tables or charts by different metrics, for personalized analysis.

- **Responsive Design**: Ensure dashboards are mobile-friendly, making them accessible from various devices.

## 2. Best Practices for Designing Interactive Dashboards

- **Clear Structure**: Organize data into logical sections or tabs for easy navigation.

- **Focus on Key Metrics**: Highlight the most important metrics or KPIs, ensuring that users can quickly identify trends and make decisions.

- **User-Friendly Interface**: Keep the design simple and intuitive, avoiding overwhelming users with too many options.

- **Real-Time Data**: Where applicable, use real-time data updates to provide users with the most up-to-date information.

## 3. Tools for Building Interactive Dashboards

- **Tableau**: Tableau allows users to create interactive dashboards with filters, drill-downs, and dynamic elements.
- **Power BI**: Power BI also provides a rich set of interactive dashboard features, including slicers, drill-throughs, and dynamic visuals.
- **Google Data Studio**: A free tool for creating interactive dashboards with integration into Google products and services.
- **D3.js**: For more complex and fully customized interactive visualizations on the web.

---

### *Real-World Example: Data Visualization for Marketing Campaigns*

Data visualization plays a crucial role in **marketing analytics**, allowing businesses to track the effectiveness of their campaigns and make data-driven decisions. Let's consider a real-world example of how a company might use data visualization to analyze a **marketing campaign**.

### Campaign Data Collection

An e-commerce company runs a marketing campaign promoting a new product. The company collects various data points related to the campaign:

- **Website Traffic**: Number of visitors, time spent on the site, pages viewed.
- **Ad Click-Through Rate (CTR)**: Number of clicks on online ads divided by the number of impressions.
- **Conversion Rate**: Percentage of visitors who make a purchase after clicking on the ad.
- **Social Media Engagement**: Likes, shares, comments, and mentions across platforms like Facebook, Twitter, and Instagram.
- **Customer Feedback**: Survey responses and online reviews.

## Using Tableau for Marketing Analytics

The marketing team uses **Tableau** to visualize the campaign data:

- **Conversion Funnel**: A bar chart showing the percentage of users who progress from viewing the ad to making a purchase.
- **Time-Series Line Chart**: A line chart showing website traffic over the course of the campaign, highlighting key events or promotions.
- **Geographical Heatmap**: A heatmap showing sales by region, helping identify which areas responded best to the campaign.
- **Sentiment Analysis Dashboard**: A word cloud and sentiment trend graph based on customer feedback from social media and reviews.

Insights from the Visualization

- **Geographic Trends**: The heatmap shows that certain regions had higher conversion rates, indicating a more successful campaign in those areas.
- **Ad Effectiveness**: The conversion funnel reveals that although many users clicked on the ads, a significant portion did not convert into sales. The marketing team could experiment with different ad creatives or landing pages.
- **Customer Sentiment**: The sentiment analysis dashboard reveals that while customer feedback on the product was mostly positive, there were a few recurring concerns regarding shipping delays, which the team could address in future campaigns.

---

In this chapter, we explored the crucial role of **data visualization** in unlocking the value of big data. We discussed **best practices** for visualizing data, the importance of choosing the right type of visualization for different data, and the power of interactivity in dashboards. We also reviewed three popular **data visualization tools**: **Tableau**, **Power BI**, and **D3.js**, and how each is suited to different visualization needs.

Finally, we provided a **real-world example** of how an e-commerce company could use **data visualization** to assess the effectiveness of a **marketing campaign**, highlighting how actionable insights can be derived from visual representations of data.

As we move forward in the book, we will delve deeper into the **advanced techniques** for data analysis and how big data can drive innovation and decision-making in various industries.

# Chapter 10: Machine Learning and Big Data

In the era of big data, **machine learning (ML)** has become a powerful tool for extracting insights, identifying patterns, and making predictions. By analyzing large datasets, machine learning algorithms can automatically improve their performance over time without being explicitly programmed. This chapter will explore how **machine learning** complements **big data**, distinguish between **supervised** and **unsupervised learning**, discuss the process of **training models on big data**, and conclude with a **real-world example** of how **predictive analytics** in healthcare is being used to **predict disease outbreaks**.

---

### *How Machine Learning Complements Big Data*

Machine learning and big data go hand-in-hand. The large volumes of data generated from various sources—whether it's customer behavior data, sensor data, or social media posts—provide a rich foundation for training machine learning models. The power of machine learning comes from its ability to learn from large datasets, identify patterns, and make predictions or recommendations based on that data.

1. Leveraging Big Data for Machine Learning

- **Data Availability**: Big data provides a wide variety of information, enabling machine learning models to learn from diverse sources and to identify complex patterns that might not be visible in smaller datasets.

- **Improved Accuracy**: With more data, machine learning models can become more accurate over time. For example, a recommendation system can improve its suggestions as it learns more about customer preferences.

- **Real-Time Insights**: Big data allows for the integration of real-time data streams, which can be used to continuously update machine learning models and provide up-to-date insights.

## 2. The Role of Machine Learning in Big Data Analytics

Machine learning can analyze large datasets to:

- **Predict trends**: For example, forecasting sales based on historical data.

- **Automate tasks**: For example, classifying documents or emails into predefined categories.

- **Uncover hidden patterns**: For example, identifying previously unknown customer behaviors that could inform business strategies.

In big data environments, traditional methods of analysis often fall short because of the volume, variety, and velocity of data. Machine learning, however, is well-suited to handle these challenges, enabling organizations to unlock deeper insights and make data-driven decisions more effectively.

---

### *Supervised vs. Unsupervised Learning*

In machine learning, models can be categorized into two main types based on how they learn from the data: **supervised learning** and **unsupervised learning**.

### 1. Supervised Learning

In supervised learning, the model is trained on labeled data, meaning that the input data is paired with the correct output. The goal is for the model to learn the mapping from inputs to outputs, so it can predict the output for new, unseen data.

- **Example**: Predicting house prices based on features such as square footage, number of bedrooms, and location. The dataset would include both the features and the corresponding house prices, which allows the model to learn the relationship between them.
- **Common Algorithms**:
    - **Linear Regression**: Used for predicting continuous values.
    - **Logistic Regression**: Used for binary classification tasks (e.g., spam vs. non-spam).

- o **Decision Trees**: Used for classification and regression tasks.
  - o **Support Vector Machines (SVM)**: Used for classification tasks.
- **Applications**:
  - o **Fraud detection**: Predicting whether a transaction is fraudulent based on past transaction data.
  - o **Customer churn prediction**: Predicting whether a customer will leave a service based on historical data.

## 2. Unsupervised Learning

In unsupervised learning, the model is given unlabeled data and must find patterns or structures in the data on its own. Unlike supervised learning, there is no "correct answer" for the model to learn from. The goal is typically to identify hidden patterns or groupings in the data.

- **Example**: Customer segmentation, where the model groups customers based on purchasing behavior without knowing beforehand what the groupings should be.
- **Common Algorithms**:
  - o **K-means Clustering**: A method for grouping data points into clusters based on similarity.
  - o **Hierarchical Clustering**: Builds a tree of clusters and is useful for hierarchical relationships.

- o **Principal Component Analysis (PCA)**: Used for dimensionality reduction by identifying the most important features of the data.
- **Applications**:
  - o **Market segmentation**: Identifying distinct groups of customers to tailor marketing strategies.
  - o **Anomaly detection**: Detecting unusual patterns or outliers in data, such as identifying fraudulent transactions.

**Key Differences:**

| Aspect | Supervised Learning | Unsupervised Learning |
|---|---|---|
| **Data** | Labeled data (inputs and corresponding outputs) | Unlabeled data (no predefined output) |
| **Goal** | Learn a mapping from inputs to outputs | Discover hidden patterns or structures in the data |
| **Example** | Predicting stock prices based on historical data | Clustering customers based on purchasing behavior |
| **Common Algorithms** | Linear regression, logistic regression, decision trees | K-means clustering, hierarchical clustering, PCA |

### *Training Models on Big Data*

Training machine learning models on big data requires more than just having access to large datasets; it also requires the right tools, techniques, and infrastructure. The main challenges when training models on big data include **scalability**, **data storage**, and **computation power**.

### 1. Scalability

To scale machine learning models on big data, we need to leverage distributed computing frameworks, such as **Apache Spark** or **Hadoop**, to handle the data across multiple machines or nodes. These frameworks allow the data to be processed in parallel, speeding up the training process.

- **Spark MLlib**: Spark's machine learning library enables large-scale machine learning algorithms to be run on distributed data, making it possible to train models on massive datasets.
- **TensorFlow**: A deep learning framework that supports distributed training on large datasets across multiple machines or GPUs.

### 2. Feature Engineering and Data Preprocessing

Before training a model, it is crucial to preprocess and engineer the data appropriately. Feature engineering involves selecting the most relevant features and transforming them into a format suitable for machine learning algorithms.

- **Normalization** and **Standardization** of features.
- Handling **missing data** and **outliers**.
- Creating new features that could improve model performance.

### 3. Model Training

- **Batch Processing**: When training models on large datasets, it's often necessary to process data in batches, especially when the dataset is too large to fit into memory all at once.
- **Real-Time Processing**: For applications requiring real-time predictions (e.g., fraud detection), stream processing frameworks like **Apache Kafka** can be used to train models incrementally as data arrives.

### 4. Model Evaluation

Once a model is trained, it's important to evaluate its performance. This involves using techniques like **cross-validation**, **confusion matrices**, and evaluation metrics such as **accuracy**, **precision**, **recall**, and **F1 score**.

---

***Real-World Example: Predictive Analytics in Healthcare (Predicting Disease Outbreaks)***

Predictive analytics using machine learning is increasingly being used in the **healthcare industry** to predict and prevent **disease outbreaks**. By analyzing historical health data, social media trends, and environmental factors, machine learning models can help identify potential outbreaks before they happen.

## 1. Data Collection for Disease Prediction

- **Historical Health Data**: Data from previous outbreaks, including symptoms, locations, and time frames.
- **Social Media and News**: Analyzing social media posts and news reports to track the emergence of disease-related conversations and potential outbreaks.
- **Weather and Environmental Data**: Temperature, humidity, and other environmental factors that may affect disease transmission.

## 2. Machine Learning in Action

Machine learning models can be trained on this data to predict the likelihood of an outbreak in a given region. For example:

- **Supervised Learning**: A model can be trained using past outbreaks (labeled data) to predict the occurrence of future outbreaks based on environmental conditions, healthcare records, and social media activity.
- **Unsupervised Learning**: Cluster similar regions based on disease patterns to identify areas at high risk for outbreaks.

## 3. Outcome

By applying machine learning to healthcare data, predictive models can:

- **Identify at-risk areas**: Predict potential disease hotspots based on patterns and environmental data.
- **Alert health organizations**: Provide early warnings to public health officials, allowing them to respond proactively.
- **Optimize resource allocation**: Direct resources, such as vaccines or medical personnel, to areas that need them most.

---

In this chapter, we explored how **machine learning** complements **big data** by enabling the extraction of actionable insights from large datasets. We discussed the differences between **supervised** and **unsupervised learning**, and how each type of learning is applied to big data scenarios. We also covered the process of **training machine learning models** on big data, highlighting the challenges and solutions for scalability, preprocessing, and evaluation.

Finally, we examined a **real-world example** in healthcare, where **predictive analytics** is used to predict disease outbreaks. This example demonstrated the power of machine learning to improve public health outcomes by using big data to make proactive decisions.

As we continue, we will explore how machine learning can be applied to solve complex problems across various industries, leveraging big data to drive innovation and better decision-making.

# Chapter 11: Big Data Analytics

In the world of big data, analytics plays a crucial role in unlocking valuable insights that drive decision-making and business strategies. **Big data analytics** involves the use of advanced analytical techniques to explore, analyze, and interpret large volumes of data in real time or in batches. In this chapter, we will explore the different types of analytics—**descriptive**, **predictive**, and **prescriptive**—and look at the tools available for big data analytics, such as **Apache Flink** and **Apache Storm**. We will also discuss the differences between **real-time analytics** and **batch processing** and conclude with a **real-world example** of how big data analytics is applied in **sports** to analyze **player performance**.

---

### *Descriptive, Predictive, and Prescriptive Analytics*

The three primary types of analytics—**descriptive**, **predictive**, and **prescriptive**—serve different purposes and are applied at different stages of the decision-making process. Each type helps organizations derive valuable insights from big data.

### 1. Descriptive Analytics

Descriptive analytics is the process of summarizing historical data to understand what has happened in the past. This type of analytics helps organizations understand trends, patterns, and relationships within data. Descriptive analytics often involves basic statistical methods, aggregations, and visualizations.

- **What it Does**:
    - o Provides a summary of past events.
    - o Identifies trends, patterns, and anomalies.
    - o Answers questions like "What happened?" and "What is the current state of affairs?"
- **Examples**:
    - o Analyzing sales data over the past quarter to understand revenue trends.
    - o Examining website traffic to identify which pages have the highest visits.
- **Tools**: Descriptive analytics often uses business intelligence tools like **Tableau**, **Power BI**, and **Excel**, which aggregate data and provide dashboards, reports, and visualizations.

## 2. Predictive Analytics

Predictive analytics goes beyond historical data to forecast future events. It uses statistical models, machine learning algorithms, and data mining techniques to make predictions about future outcomes based on past data.

- **What it Does**:
    - o Analyzes historical data to predict future trends and behaviors.

- o Answers questions like "What is likely to happen?" and "What are the chances of a specific outcome?"
- **Examples**:
  - o Predicting customer churn based on historical data about customer behavior.
  - o Forecasting sales based on seasonal trends and past sales data.
- **Tools**: Predictive analytics often uses machine learning libraries and tools like **scikit-learn**, **TensorFlow**, and **Apache Spark**.

## 3. Prescriptive Analytics

Prescriptive analytics provides actionable recommendations by analyzing data and suggesting the best course of action. It uses advanced techniques such as optimization algorithms, simulation, and decision analysis to recommend actions that will lead to the desired outcomes.

- **What it Does**:
  - o Offers recommendations for future actions.
  - o Answers questions like "What should we do?" and "What is the best course of action?"
- **Examples**:
  - o Recommending inventory levels for a retail business based on demand forecasts and supply chain constraints.

- o Suggesting pricing strategies based on customer demand, competitor prices, and market conditions.
- **Tools**: Prescriptive analytics uses optimization and simulation tools such as **IBM CPLEX, Google OR-Tools**, and **AIMMS**.

---

### *Tools for Big Data Analytics: Apache Flink, Apache Storm*

To process and analyze big data efficiently, several distributed data processing frameworks are available. These tools allow organizations to process large datasets in real time or in batches and perform advanced analytics on big data.

### 1. Apache Flink

**Apache Flink** is an open-source, stream-processing framework designed for high-throughput and low-latency data processing. It is particularly well-suited for **real-time analytics**.

- **Key Features**:
  - o **Stream and Batch Processing**: Flink supports both stream and batch processing, making it versatile for different types of big data workloads.
  - o **Fault Tolerance**: Flink ensures data consistency and resilience by providing exactly-once processing semantics, even in the event of failures.

- o **Stateful Processing**: Flink supports stateful operations, which allow for complex data transformations and aggregations over time.
- o **Windowing**: Flink supports windowing functions that allow data to be processed in time-bound slices, which is crucial for time-series data analysis.

- **Use Cases**:
  - o **Real-Time Analytics**: Processing real-time data streams, such as website clicks or sensor data.
  - o **Fraud Detection**: Analyzing real-time financial transactions to identify fraudulent activity.

## 2. Apache Storm

**Apache Storm** is another open-source, distributed real-time computation system designed for processing large streams of data. Storm provides low-latency processing, making it suitable for real-time analytics applications.

- **Key Features**:
  - o **Real-Time Processing**: Storm processes data in real time, making it ideal for applications where quick insights are critical.
  - o **Scalability**: Storm is designed to scale horizontally by adding more workers to handle increased data loads.

- o **Simple Programming Model**: Storm uses a simple programming model to define data processing workflows.
- **Use Cases**:
  - o **Real-Time Data Processing**: Storm is often used for real-time data processing in applications like recommendation engines, monitoring systems, and social media analytics.
  - o **Data Enrichment**: Enhancing real-time data streams by combining them with additional data sources.

## Comparing Flink and Storm

While both **Apache Flink** and **Apache Storm** are used for real-time stream processing, Flink is generally favored for complex event processing and stateful operations, while Storm is known for its simplicity and low-latency processing.

| Feature | Apache Flink | Apache Storm |
| --- | --- | --- |
| **Data Processing** | Stream and batch processing | Real-time stream processing |
| **State Management** | Stateful processing with advanced windowing | Stateless processing, simple data transformations |

| Feature | Apache Flink | Apache Storm |
|---|---|---|
| Fault Tolerance | Exactly-once processing semantics | At-least-once processing semantics |
| Scalability | Horizontal scaling | Horizontal scaling |
| Complexity | More complex to configure but powerful for complex tasks | Easier to set up and deploy, suitable for simple tasks |

## Real-World Example: Big Data Analytics in Sports (Player Performance Analysis)

In the world of sports, big data analytics has become essential for improving player performance, optimizing team strategies, and enhancing fan engagement. **Player performance analysis** is one area where big data is increasingly being applied, with teams and coaches relying on data to make decisions on everything from training programs to in-game strategies.

### 1. Data Collection

- **Player Statistics**: Teams collect data on player performance, including metrics such as speed, distance covered, shot accuracy, and player positioning during games.

- **Wearable Devices**: Players wear sensors that track their physical movements, heart rate, and fatigue levels during training and games.
- **Video Analysis**: Video feeds of games are analyzed to track player movements, interactions with teammates, and opponent strategies.

## 2. Analyzing Player Performance with Big Data

Big data analytics is used to track individual player performance over time and identify trends or areas for improvement:

- **Descriptive Analytics**: Summarizing player statistics to understand performance trends (e.g., average speed per game, shots made vs. shots taken).
- **Predictive Analytics**: Forecasting player performance based on historical data, such as predicting how a player will perform in future games given certain conditions.
- **Prescriptive Analytics**: Recommending training modifications, rest schedules, or tactical changes based on performance data to optimize future performance.

## 3. Real-Time Performance Monitoring

- **Real-Time Analytics**: During a game, real-time analytics can be used to monitor player performance, track fatigue levels, and provide immediate feedback to coaches.

- **Wearables and IoT**: Real-time data collected from wearables can be streamed and analyzed using platforms like **Apache Flink** or **Apache Storm** to provide coaches with immediate insights into player condition.

## 4. Optimizing Team Strategy

By analyzing data on individual player performance, coaches can adjust strategies and make tactical decisions, such as:

- **Substitution Patterns**: Deciding when to substitute players based on fatigue levels or performance metrics.
- **Game Strategy**: Adjusting defensive or offensive strategies based on how players are performing in real time.

## 5. Outcome

- **Improved Performance**: By using big data to identify performance gaps and areas for improvement, players can tailor their training regimens, leading to better individual and team performance.
- **Competitive Advantage**: Teams using data-driven insights gain a competitive edge by making more informed decisions on player training, strategy, and in-game performance.

In this chapter, we explored **big data analytics** and its various applications in helping organizations derive actionable insights from large datasets. We discussed the three primary types of analytics—**descriptive**, **predictive**, and **prescriptive**—and how they help organizations answer different questions. We also reviewed two powerful tools for big data analytics, **Apache Flink** and **Apache Storm**, which enable real-time and batch processing of large datasets.

Finally, we presented a **real-world example** of how **big data analytics** is used in **sports** to analyze **player performance**, demonstrating how predictive and prescriptive analytics can optimize training, improve team strategy, and enhance overall performance.

As we continue, we will delve deeper into how big data analytics can be applied across industries like healthcare, finance, and marketing, driving innovation and improving decision-making at every level.

# Chapter 12: Artificial Intelligence and Big Data

Artificial Intelligence (AI) and Big Data are transforming industries across the globe, with AI providing the capability to process, interpret, and make decisions based on large volumes of complex data. The synergy between **AI** and **Big Data** enables organizations to leverage data for deeper insights, predictions, and automation. In this chapter, we will explore the **role of AI in big data processing**, examine **AI and machine learning algorithms** used to analyze big data, discuss **deep learning and neural networks** in the context of big data, and conclude with a **real-world example** of how **AI** is applied in **autonomous vehicles**.

---

### *The Role of AI in Big Data Processing*

The convergence of **AI** and **big data** brings immense value by enabling machines to learn from data, uncover hidden patterns, and make decisions without human intervention. Big data often involves vast amounts of structured and unstructured information, and AI provides the tools to process and analyze this data at scale, turning raw data into actionable insights.

1. Enhancing Data Processing with AI

AI enhances big data processing by automating data analysis tasks that would otherwise require manual effort or traditional computational methods. AI-driven techniques can:

- **Clean and preprocess data**: AI can identify missing values, outliers, and anomalies in data, streamlining the data cleaning process.
- **Automate data interpretation**: AI models can analyze vast datasets and derive insights far faster than traditional methods.
- **Extract meaningful patterns**: AI uses advanced algorithms to identify trends and patterns that are difficult for humans to detect.

## 2. AI for Decision-Making

In the realm of big data, AI helps organizations make data-driven decisions. By continuously analyzing data streams and identifying correlations, AI can:

- **Provide real-time insights**: AI can analyze real-time data from various sources (e.g., IoT devices, social media) and generate insights to help organizations act on them immediately.
- **Support automation**: AI algorithms can automate decision-making processes, such as adjusting marketing strategies or altering production schedules based on real-time data.

## *AI and Machine Learning Algorithms for Big Data*

Machine Learning (ML), a subset of AI, is particularly powerful when dealing with big data. ML algorithms enable computers to learn from large datasets and improve their performance over time without being explicitly programmed.

## 1. Supervised Learning for Big Data

In supervised learning, the model is trained on labeled data, with input-output pairs used to teach the algorithm how to map inputs to correct outputs. Supervised learning algorithms can be applied to big data in a variety of domains:

- **Classification**: Predicting categorical outcomes (e.g., spam detection, sentiment analysis).
- **Regression**: Predicting continuous outcomes (e.g., price prediction, forecasting sales).
- **Popular Algorithms**:
  - **Linear Regression**: For continuous prediction.
  - **Decision Trees**: Used for classification and regression tasks.
  - **Random Forest**: A more powerful ensemble method based on decision trees.
  - **Support Vector Machines (SVM)**: Often used for classification problems in high-dimensional datasets.

## 2. Unsupervised Learning for Big Data

Unsupervised learning is used when the data is not labeled. The model tries to identify inherent patterns or structures within the data, such as clustering similar data points or reducing the dimensionality of the data.

- **Popular Algorithms**:
    - o **K-Means Clustering**: A method for grouping data points into clusters based on similarity.
    - o **Principal Component Analysis (PCA)**: A technique for reducing the dimensionality of the data while retaining as much variability as possible.
    - o **Hierarchical Clustering**: A method for creating a tree-like structure to represent relationships between data points.

## 3. Reinforcement Learning for Big Data

Reinforcement learning (RL) is another branch of machine learning where an agent learns how to act in an environment by performing actions and receiving feedback in the form of rewards or penalties.

- **Applications**: RL can be used for applications like game-playing, robotics, and recommendation systems, where an agent interacts with the environment to optimize a certain objective.

*Deep Learning and Neural Networks for Big Data*

Deep learning, a subset of machine learning, is inspired by the structure and function of the human brain and is designed to handle complex tasks such as image recognition, speech processing, and natural language understanding. **Neural networks**, the foundation of deep learning, are made up of layers of interconnected nodes (or neurons) that process information in a manner similar to how neurons in the human brain work.

## 1. The Basics of Neural Networks

A neural network consists of:

- **Input Layer**: Where data enters the network.
- **Hidden Layers**: Layers that process the data by applying weights and activation functions.
- **Output Layer**: The final prediction or classification result.

Deep learning models often involve multiple hidden layers, creating **deep neural networks** (DNNs), which are capable of learning highly complex representations of data.

## 2. Convolutional Neural Networks (CNNs)

CNNs are a specific type of neural network used primarily for **image processing**. They are designed to automatically and adaptively learn spatial hierarchies of features from images, making them ideal for visual tasks such as object detection and image classification.

- **Applications**: Image recognition, facial recognition, autonomous vehicles.

### 3. Recurrent Neural Networks (RNNs)

RNNs are designed for sequence data and are used in applications where time or sequential dependencies matter, such as **speech recognition** and **natural language processing**.

- **Applications**: Time series forecasting, text generation, language translation.

### 4. Training Deep Learning Models on Big Data

Training deep learning models requires significant computational resources due to the complexity of the models and the massive amounts of data involved. Big data platforms, such as **TensorFlow** and **PyTorch**, provide scalable tools to train deep learning models on large datasets.

- **GPU Acceleration**: Graphics Processing Units (GPUs) are often used to accelerate deep learning training processes due to their ability to handle parallel computations efficiently.
- **Cloud Computing**: Cloud platforms such as **Google Cloud**, **AWS**, and **Microsoft Azure** provide the computational power required for training large deep learning models.

*Real-World Example: AI in Autonomous Vehicles*

One of the most exciting applications of AI and big data is in **autonomous vehicles**, where AI is used to process massive amounts of data from sensors, cameras, and other devices to make real-time decisions about how the vehicle should navigate its environment.

## 1. Data Collection in Autonomous Vehicles

Autonomous vehicles rely on a variety of sensors and devices to collect real-time data about the vehicle's surroundings, including:

- **LIDAR**: A laser-based sensor used for mapping and measuring distances.
- **Cameras**: For visual recognition, including identifying road signs, obstacles, and lane markings.
- **Radar**: For detecting objects and measuring speed.
- **GPS**: For location tracking and route planning.

This data is processed in real-time to create a model of the vehicle's environment, enabling the vehicle to make informed decisions about its next move.

## 2. AI and Machine Learning in Autonomous Vehicles

AI and machine learning algorithms are used to process and analyze the data collected by the vehicle's sensors. Some of the key tasks include:

- **Object Detection**: Identifying pedestrians, other vehicles, traffic signs, and obstacles in the vehicle's path using **deep learning** techniques, such as **convolutional neural networks (CNNs)**.

- **Path Planning**: Using **reinforcement learning (RL)** to determine the most efficient and safest route based on real-time data.

- **Decision-Making**: AI algorithms combine input from sensors and map data to make decisions, such as when to stop at a red light, avoid an obstacle, or merge onto a highway.

## 3. Deep Learning in Autonomous Vehicles

Deep learning models are essential for recognizing complex patterns in visual data, such as distinguishing between a pedestrian and a cyclist, or identifying road signs in different weather conditions. These models are trained on vast datasets of images and sensor data to improve their accuracy over time.

## 4. Real-Time Data Processing

Autonomous vehicles require real-time data processing to make immediate decisions. Systems like **Apache Kafka**, **Apache Flink**, and **Apache Storm** are used for real-time data streaming and analysis, ensuring that the vehicle can respond instantly to changes in its environment.

## 5. Challenges and Future of AI in Autonomous Vehicles

- **Data Privacy**: Autonomous vehicles generate vast amounts of personal data, such as location tracking, raising privacy concerns.

- **Safety and Reliability**: Ensuring that AI models are reliable and can make safe decisions in complex, real-world scenarios is critical.

- **Regulatory Compliance**: Governments are still working on frameworks for regulating autonomous vehicles and ensuring their safe integration into public roads.

In this chapter, we explored how **AI** plays a critical role in **big data processing**, from enhancing data analysis to enabling real-time decision-making. We discussed the differences between **supervised** and **unsupervised learning**, and examined how deep learning and neural networks contribute to the handling of complex big data tasks. Additionally, we explored a **real-world example** of how **AI** is used in **autonomous vehicles** to process sensor data, make real-time decisions, and navigate complex environments.

As AI continues to evolve, its integration with big data will only become more sophisticated, enabling groundbreaking applications across industries such as healthcare, finance, transportation, and entertainment. In the next chapters, we will dive deeper into specific applications of AI and explore how they can be implemented to solve real-world problems.

# Chapter 13: Big Data Security and Privacy

As big data becomes increasingly integral to business operations, the security and privacy of the data are paramount. Organizations are tasked with safeguarding sensitive data from breaches, unauthorized access, and misuse while ensuring compliance with regulations. In this chapter, we will explore how to **protect sensitive data** in the big data era, discuss the importance of **data encryption** and **access control**, and explore **data anonymization** as a privacy measure. We will conclude with a **real-world example** of the **security challenges** faced in the context of **financial data**.

---

### *Protecting Sensitive Data in the Big Data Era*

In the age of big data, protecting sensitive data is increasingly challenging due to the sheer volume, variety, and velocity of information being collected. Data security involves both the **technical** and **organizational** measures required to prevent unauthorized access and ensure the integrity and confidentiality of the data.

### 1. The Challenges of Big Data Security

- **Data Breaches**: With large amounts of data being stored and processed, the risk of data breaches increases. Attackers may target databases, cloud storage, or data pipelines to access sensitive information.

- **Distributed Data**: Big data often involves storing and processing data across multiple locations (on-premises, cloud, hybrid environments). This creates challenges in ensuring that security policies are consistently applied across all platforms.
- **Data Sharing**: In many big data applications, data is shared among different departments or external partners, increasing the potential for accidental or intentional data leakage.

## 2. Regulatory Compliance and Data Protection

- **GDPR**: The **General Data Protection Regulation (GDPR)** in the European Union imposes strict rules on how organizations must handle and protect personal data.
- **HIPAA**: In healthcare, the **Health Insurance Portability and Accountability Act (HIPAA)** sets standards for protecting patient health information.
- **CCPA**: The **California Consumer Privacy Act (CCPA)** provides California residents with greater control over their personal data and requires businesses to take certain steps to protect that data.

Big data security requires adherence to these and other regulations to avoid fines and reputational damage.

## *Data Encryption and Access Control*

**Data encryption** and **access control** are two fundamental measures for protecting sensitive data in big data environments.

### 1. Data Encryption

Encryption converts data into a format that can only be read or decrypted by someone with the correct key. It is essential for ensuring that data remains confidential and protected, especially when it is stored or transmitted over unsecured networks.

- **Encryption at Rest**: This involves encrypting data stored on physical media (e.g., hard drives, cloud storage) to prevent unauthorized access if the storage media is compromised.
- **Encryption in Transit**: This ensures that data being transmitted over networks (e.g., between servers or between a client and a server) is encrypted to prevent interception during transmission.
- **Common Encryption Standards**:
  - **AES (Advanced Encryption Standard)**: Widely used for encrypting sensitive data.
  - **RSA**: Used for secure key exchange and digital signatures.
  - **SSL/TLS**: Used to secure data in transit, particularly for web communications.

## 2. Access Control

Access control mechanisms ensure that only authorized users and applications have access to sensitive data. Effective access control is necessary to prevent unauthorized users from gaining access to confidential or private information.

- **Role-Based Access Control (RBAC)**: In RBAC, access is granted based on the user's role within the organization. For example, a database administrator might have full access to data, while a marketing employee only has access to certain customer information.

- **Least Privilege**: Users should only be given the minimum level of access necessary to perform their tasks, reducing the risk of data misuse or breach.

- **Multi-Factor Authentication (MFA)**: Adding extra layers of authentication (such as SMS codes or biometrics) can further secure access to sensitive data systems.

## 3. Managing Permissions in Big Data

Given the large scale and complexity of big data environments, managing access to different datasets is challenging. Platforms like **Hadoop** and **Spark** offer granular permission models, allowing administrators to control access at the file, table, or even column level.

## *Ensuring Privacy with Data Anonymization*

**Data anonymization** is the process of removing personally identifiable information (PII) from datasets to ensure that individuals cannot be identified. It is an essential privacy measure, particularly when sharing or analyzing sensitive data for research or analytics purposes.

## 1. What is Data Anonymization?

Data anonymization involves altering data in such a way that it can no longer be traced back to an individual. Common anonymization techniques include:

- **Generalization**: Replacing specific values with more general categories. For example, replacing an exact age with an age range (e.g., 30-40).
- **Suppression**: Removing sensitive data fields, such as name, address, or social security number, from datasets.
- **Data Masking**: Replacing sensitive data with fictional or scrambled data that retains the same structure.

## 2. The Importance of Data Anonymization

- **Compliance**: Anonymization helps organizations comply with privacy regulations (e.g., GDPR, HIPAA) that require the protection of personal data.

- **Data Sharing**: Anonymized data can be safely shared with third parties (e.g., researchers, external partners) without exposing individual identities.

- **Risk Reduction**: By anonymizing data, organizations reduce the risk of identity theft, privacy violations, and other security concerns associated with personally identifiable data.

## 3. Anonymization vs. Pseudonymization

- **Anonymization**: Data cannot be traced back to an individual, even with additional information.

- **Pseudonymization**: Data is still identifiable through a pseudonym (e.g., an ID number), but personal details are not directly accessible. While pseudonymized data offers some level of protection, it does not provide full privacy like anonymization.

---

### Real-World Example: Security Challenges in Financial Data

In the **financial sector**, big data is used for tasks such as risk management, fraud detection, and customer analytics. However, the handling of financial data presents significant security challenges due to the highly sensitive nature of the information and the strict regulatory requirements.

## 1. Sensitive Financial Data

- **Personal Identifiable Information (PII)**: Financial institutions store personal information such as customer names, addresses, bank account numbers, and social security numbers. This data is a prime target for cybercriminals.
- **Transaction Data**: Transactions, including payments, wire transfers, and loan applications, need to be securely processed and stored.

## 2. Security Challenges in Financial Data

- **Data Breaches**: Cyberattacks, such as **SQL injection** or **ransomware**, can expose sensitive customer data. Financial institutions must implement robust security measures, including **encryption** and **multi-factor authentication**, to protect against breaches.
- **Insider Threats**: Employees with access to sensitive financial data can pose a security risk. **Role-based access control (RBAC)** and **least privilege** policies are essential for limiting internal access.
- **Third-Party Risks**: Financial institutions often share data with third-party vendors, which can introduce additional vulnerabilities. **Data anonymization** and **data encryption** are essential when sharing financial data with external parties.

## 3. Compliance with Regulations

Financial institutions must comply with regulations such as:

- **GDPR**: Requires the protection of personal data, including anonymization and encryption of customer information.
- **PCI DSS**: The **Payment Card Industry Data Security Standard** requires that financial data, such as credit card numbers, be stored securely and processed with strict access control measures.

## 4. Preventive Measures

To address security challenges, financial institutions adopt a range of best practices:

- **Encryption**: Ensuring that financial data is encrypted both at rest and in transit.
- **Access Control**: Using RBAC to limit access to sensitive financial data and implementing multi-factor authentication for high-risk operations.
- **Regular Audits**: Conducting regular security audits to detect vulnerabilities and ensure compliance with regulatory standards.

In this chapter, we explored the essential concepts of **big data security** and **privacy** in the modern data landscape. We discussed the importance of **data encryption** and **access control** in protecting sensitive data, and how **data anonymization** can help safeguard privacy while allowing data sharing and analysis. We also examined the **real-world example** of **security challenges in financial data**, highlighting the importance of robust security measures to protect financial information from breaches, fraud, and regulatory violations.

As the volume and complexity of data continue to grow, so too will the challenges associated with securing it. Organizations must continually adopt advanced technologies and best practices to ensure the confidentiality, integrity, and availability of their data, while adhering to privacy laws and protecting their customers' trust.

# Chapter 14: Cloud Computing and Big Data

Cloud computing has become a cornerstone of modern **big data** solutions, providing organizations with the flexibility, scalability, and cost-efficiency needed to handle massive datasets. By leveraging cloud platforms, businesses can easily store, process, and analyze big data without the need for expensive on-premises infrastructure. In this chapter, we will explore how **cloud computing supports big data solutions**, look at key cloud providers like **AWS**, **Azure**, and **Google Cloud**, and discuss the scalability and cost-efficiency advantages of using cloud platforms. We will conclude with a **real-world example** of how **big data** is utilized in **cloud platforms** for **retail analytics**.

---

### *How Cloud Computing Supports Big Data Solutions*

Cloud computing provides on-demand access to computing resources like storage, processing power, and networking capabilities, enabling organizations to build and scale big data solutions efficiently. Traditionally, managing big data required significant investments in physical infrastructure and hardware. Cloud computing has revolutionized this by offering the following key benefits:

## 1. Flexibility and Accessibility

- **On-Demand Resources**: Cloud services offer resources like storage, computing power, and databases that can be scaled up or down based on demand. This flexibility is crucial for big data workloads, where resource needs can vary significantly.
- **Global Accessibility**: Cloud platforms enable organizations to access data and applications from anywhere in the world. This ensures that teams can collaborate on data analysis and insights in real time, regardless of their location.

## 2. Data Storage and Management

Cloud platforms provide scalable storage solutions that are designed to handle large volumes of data, from structured data (e.g., databases) to unstructured data (e.g., social media posts, images, and videos). Examples of cloud storage services include:

- **Object Storage**: Services like **Amazon S3** or **Azure Blob Storage** allow businesses to store vast amounts of unstructured data in scalable, cost-effective storage.
- **Data Lakes**: Cloud providers offer **data lake** services, such as **AWS Lake Formation** or **Azure Data Lake**, to store raw data in its native format, making it easier to perform big data analysis.

## 3. Real-Time Data Processing

Cloud computing enables real-time data processing, which is essential for applications like fraud detection, recommendation engines, and social media analytics. Services like **AWS Lambda**, **Azure Functions**, and **Google Cloud Functions** allow organizations to process data in real time, ensuring that they can take immediate action based on insights derived from big data.

## 4. Big Data Analytics Services

Cloud platforms offer a range of big data analytics services that simplify data analysis, machine learning, and reporting. For example:

- **Amazon EMR (Elastic MapReduce)**: A cloud-native platform that processes big data using Apache Hadoop, Spark, and other frameworks.
- **Google BigQuery**: A serverless data warehouse that enables fast SQL-based analytics on large datasets.
- **Azure Synapse Analytics**: A cloud-based analytics service that integrates big data and data warehousing for seamless data analysis.

---

### *Key Cloud Providers: AWS, Azure, Google Cloud*

The three major cloud providers—**Amazon Web Services (AWS)**, **Microsoft Azure**, and **Google Cloud Platform (GCP)**—offer a variety of services tailored for big data solutions. Each provider has its strengths, and the choice of platform often depends on the specific needs of the business.

## 1. Amazon Web Services (AWS)

AWS is one of the leading cloud service providers and offers a comprehensive suite of tools for big data, including storage, computing, and analytics services.

- **Key Big Data Services**:
  - **Amazon S3**: Scalable object storage for storing data.
  - **Amazon EMR**: Managed Hadoop and Spark service for processing big data.
  - **Amazon Redshift**: A fast, scalable data warehouse for analyzing large datasets.
  - **AWS Glue**: A serverless data integration service for preparing and transforming data.
- **Strengths**:
  - **Comprehensive Ecosystem**: AWS offers a wide array of services, making it suitable for businesses with complex big data needs.
  - **Scalability**: AWS services are designed to scale with your data, from small datasets to petabytes of data.

## 2. Microsoft Azure

Azure is another major player in the cloud space and provides a range of big data services, along with deep integration with Microsoft's suite of enterprise software.

- **Key Big Data Services**:
    - o **Azure Blob Storage**: Scalable object storage for unstructured data.
    - o **Azure Data Lake**: A cloud-based data lake for storing large amounts of raw data.
    - o **Azure Synapse Analytics**: A unified analytics platform for big data and data warehousing.
    - o **Azure Databricks**: An Apache Spark-based analytics platform for big data processing.
- **Strengths**:
    - o **Integration with Microsoft Tools**: Azure seamlessly integrates with Microsoft products such as Office 365, Power BI, and SQL Server.
    - o **Hybrid Cloud Solutions**: Azure is known for its hybrid cloud capabilities, allowing businesses to run workloads across both on-premises and cloud environments.

## 3. Google Cloud Platform (GCP)

Google Cloud is well-known for its data analytics and machine learning capabilities, making it a popular choice for big data processing and analysis.

- **Key Big Data Services**:
  - ○ **Google Cloud Storage**: Scalable storage for unstructured data.
  - ○ **BigQuery**: A fully managed, serverless data warehouse for fast, SQL-based analytics.
  - ○ **Google Cloud Dataproc**: A managed Spark and Hadoop service for big data processing.
  - ○ **Google AI Platform**: A suite of machine learning tools for building and deploying models on big data.
- **Strengths**:
  - ○ **Data Analytics**: Google Cloud is particularly strong in data analytics and machine learning, thanks to tools like BigQuery and Google AI.
  - ○ **Serverless Solutions**: Google Cloud provides serverless computing options that allow businesses to scale without managing infrastructure.

*Scalability and Cost Efficiency in the Cloud*

Cloud platforms offer **scalability** and **cost efficiency**, two of the most important advantages for businesses working with big data.

1. Scalability

Cloud platforms allow businesses to scale their infrastructure and resources in real-time to accommodate changing data needs. Whether you need to scale up to handle a data surge or scale down during periods of low activity, cloud services offer the flexibility to adjust resources quickly.

- **Elasticity**: Cloud computing offers elastic resources, meaning you only pay for what you use. For example, AWS allows you to scale services such as **Amazon EC2** (compute power) up or down based on demand.
- **Auto-scaling**: Most cloud platforms support auto-scaling, allowing applications and services to automatically adjust based on workload or traffic.

## 2. Cost Efficiency

Cloud computing reduces the need for businesses to invest heavily in physical infrastructure, offering a pay-as-you-go pricing model that allows companies to only pay for the resources they use. This helps reduce upfront costs and allows businesses to allocate their budgets more efficiently.

- **Cost Optimization**: Cloud services like **AWS Cost Explorer**, **Azure Cost Management**, and **Google Cloud Cost Management** allow businesses to track and optimize their usage and costs.
- **Serverless Computing**: Cloud platforms offer **serverless** options, such as **AWS Lambda** and **Google Cloud Functions**, which allow businesses to run code without managing servers, further reducing costs.

*Real-World Example: Big Data in Cloud Platforms for Retail Analytics*

One of the most powerful applications of big data in the cloud is in the **retail industry**, where companies can leverage cloud platforms to analyze customer behavior, optimize inventory, and personalize marketing efforts. Let's consider how a major retail brand could use **AWS**, **Azure**, or **Google Cloud** to perform **retail analytics**.

## 1. Data Collection and Storage

The retailer collects vast amounts of data from various sources:

- **Point-of-Sale (POS) Systems**: Transactional data from in-store purchases.
- **Online Transactions**: E-commerce activity, including product views, add-to-cart actions, and completed purchases.
- **Customer Interaction Data**: Social media posts, email responses, and customer service interactions.
- **IoT Devices**: Smart shelves, temperature sensors, and RFID tags that track inventory and store conditions.

This data is stored in scalable cloud storage systems such as **Amazon S3, Azure Blob Storage**, or **Google Cloud Storage**.

## 2. Data Processing and Analysis

Once the data is stored, it is processed and analyzed using cloud-based analytics services:

- **Customer Segmentation**: Retailers can use machine learning algorithms to segment customers based on behavior, purchasing patterns, and demographics.
- **Inventory Optimization**: Big data analytics can help forecast demand for specific products and optimize inventory levels across different store locations, ensuring stock availability and reducing excess inventory.
- **Personalized Recommendations**: By analyzing purchase history and browsing behavior, retailers can use machine learning models to recommend products to customers in real-time, both online and in-store.

## 3. Real-Time Analytics

Cloud platforms allow the retailer to analyze real-time data, such as tracking customer behavior as they shop. Using tools like **Google BigQuery** for analytics or **AWS Lambda** for real-time event-driven processing, the retailer can:

- **Track customer activity**: Provide personalized offers based on browsing behavior or loyalty status.
- **Monitor sales performance**: Evaluate sales trends in real time to identify high-performing products and adjust marketing strategies.

## 4. Visualizing Insights

The retailer can visualize these insights using cloud-based dashboards and reporting tools like **Tableau**, **Power BI**, or **Google Data Studio**, allowing decision-makers to monitor key metrics such as sales performance, customer engagement, and inventory turnover in real-time.

---

In this chapter, we explored how **cloud computing** supports **big data solutions** by providing scalable, flexible, and cost-efficient resources for storing, processing, and analyzing large datasets. We discussed the key cloud providers—**AWS**, **Azure**, and **Google Cloud**—and the big data services they offer, including data storage, analytics, and machine learning tools. Additionally, we highlighted the **scalability** and **cost efficiency** of cloud platforms, making them ideal for big data workloads.

Finally, we provided a **real-world example** of how cloud platforms are used for **retail analytics**, demonstrating how big data can be leveraged in the cloud to optimize inventory, personalize customer experiences, and enhance business decision-making.

As businesses continue to leverage big data in the cloud, the potential for innovation, efficiency, and cost savings will only grow, driving smarter decision-making across industries.

# Chapter 15: Real-Time Data and Streaming Analytics

As organizations increasingly rely on big data for decision-making, the ability to process and analyze data in real time has become a significant advantage. **Real-time data processing** enables businesses to act on insights instantly, enhancing customer experiences, improving operational efficiency, and driving innovation. In this chapter, we will explore the differences between **real-time data processing** and **batch processing**, review **tools for real-time analytics** such as **Apache Kafka** and **Apache Flink**, and discuss the importance of **stream processing** for big data applications. We will conclude with a **real-world example** of **real-time social media analytics**.

---

### *Real-Time Data Processing vs. Batch Processing*

Data processing can broadly be categorized into two types: **real-time** and **batch processing**. Understanding the distinction between these two approaches is essential for choosing the right technique for a given application.

### 1. Real-Time Data Processing

Real-time data processing involves analyzing data as it is generated or ingested. In this approach, data is processed immediately, with minimal delay, enabling businesses to make decisions based on the most current information available.

- **Key Characteristics**:
  - o **Low Latency**: Data is processed in real time with minimal delay.
  - o **Continuous Data Flow**: Data is constantly being generated and processed in streams.
  - o **Immediate Action**: Insights are delivered in near real-time, allowing organizations to act instantly.
- **Use Cases**:
  - o **Fraud detection**: Analyzing financial transactions in real time to detect potentially fraudulent activity.
  - o **Recommendation systems**: Providing personalized product recommendations based on current user behavior.
  - o **Operational monitoring**: Monitoring sensor data from machines or equipment to detect failures or anomalies.

## 2. Batch Processing

Batch processing refers to processing data in large, fixed-sized chunks or batches, typically at scheduled intervals (e.g., daily, weekly). This method is more suitable for large-scale data that does not require immediate analysis.

- **Key Characteristics**:
  - o **High Latency**: Data is processed in bulk after it has been accumulated.
  - o **Scheduled Processing**: Batches are processed at predefined intervals.
  - o **Data Volume**: Batch processing is ideal for scenarios where the volume of data is too large to be processed in real time.
- **Use Cases**:
  - o **End-of-day reporting**: Generating daily reports on sales, inventory, or financial transactions.
  - o **Data warehousing**: Processing historical data to perform in-depth analysis or run complex queries.
  - o **Data migration**: Moving large datasets from one system to another in periodic intervals.

## Key Differences

| Aspect | Real-Time Data Processing | Batch Processing |
|---|---|---|
| **Data Processing** | Immediate processing of continuous data streams | Processing of data in predefined chunks at intervals |

| Aspect | Real-Time Data Processing | Batch Processing |
|---|---|---|
| Latency | Low latency, near-instant processing | High latency, processing happens in intervals |
| Use Cases | Fraud detection, real-time monitoring, recommendation engines | End-of-day reports, data warehousing, batch jobs |
| Tools | Apache Kafka, Apache Flink, Google Cloud Pub/Sub | Hadoop, Apache Spark (for batch processing) |

Real-time data processing is particularly beneficial in environments where timely decisions are critical, such as finance, healthcare, and retail. Batch processing, on the other hand, is more suited to situations where immediate decisions are not necessary, but large datasets need to be processed efficiently.

---

### Tools for Real-Time Analytics: Apache Kafka, Apache Flink

Real-time data processing relies on specialized tools and platforms that can handle high volumes of streaming data. Two of the most popular tools for real-time analytics are **Apache Kafka** and **Apache Flink**.

## 1. Apache Kafka

**Apache Kafka** is an open-source distributed event streaming platform designed for building real-time data pipelines and streaming applications. Kafka is commonly used for handling large volumes of real-time data and is widely adopted for event-driven architectures.

- **Key Features**:
    - **Publish-Subscribe Model**: Kafka allows producers to send messages (events) to topics, which consumers can then subscribe to and process.
    - **Scalability**: Kafka can handle massive volumes of data by distributing it across multiple partitions and brokers.
    - **Fault Tolerance**: Kafka ensures durability by replicating messages across multiple servers.
    - **Stream Processing**: Kafka integrates with stream processing tools such as **Apache Flink** and **Kafka Streams** to process data as it flows through the system.
- **Use Cases**:
    - **Real-Time Analytics**: Stream processing and analytics on real-time data, such as monitoring website traffic or analyzing customer behavior.

- ○ **Log Aggregation**: Collecting and aggregating logs from various services for analysis and troubleshooting.
- ○ **Data Integration**: Building real-time data pipelines that connect various data sources to analytics tools or databases.

## 2. Apache Flink

**Apache Flink** is a powerful open-source stream processing framework designed for processing large-scale data streams with low latency. Unlike batch processing systems, Flink processes data as it is ingested and provides powerful features for real-time analytics.

- **Key Features**:
  - ○ **Low-Latency Processing**: Flink processes data in real time with minimal delay.
  - ○ **Stateful Processing**: Flink supports stateful stream processing, allowing applications to maintain and process state over time.
  - ○ **Event Time Processing**: Flink allows processing based on event timestamps rather than processing time, which is important for dealing with out-of-order events.

- o **Fault Tolerance**: Flink provides exactly-once semantics for reliable data processing, ensuring that data is processed without duplication or loss.
- **Use Cases**:
  - o **Real-Time Analytics**: Analyzing streaming data in real time, such as monitoring financial transactions or social media feeds.
  - o **Event-Driven Applications**: Building applications that respond to real-time events, such as recommendation systems or fraud detection systems.
  - o **IoT Data Processing**: Processing data from Internet of Things (IoT) sensors in real time to track device health or environmental conditions.

## Comparison Between Kafka and Flink

| Aspect | Apache Kafka | Apache Flink |
|---|---|---|
| **Purpose** | Event streaming platform for message distribution | Stream processing framework for real-time data analytics |
| **Use Cases** | Event-driven architectures, real-time data pipelines | Complex event processing, real-time analytics |

| Aspect | Apache Kafka | Apache Flink |
|--------|--------------|--------------|
| **Latency** | Low latency, but more suitable for event transport | Extremely low latency for stream processing |
| **Fault Tolerance** | Strong durability and replication | Exactly-once stateful processing semantics |
| **Integration** | Integrates with stream processors (e.g., Flink, Spark) | Integrates with Kafka for stream processing |

Both Kafka and Flink are often used together, with Kafka handling the event streaming and Flink processing the data in real time.

---

## *Stream Processing for Big Data Applications*

Stream processing is essential for big data applications where timely insights are critical. Stream processing frameworks like **Apache Kafka** and **Apache Flink** provide the infrastructure needed to process data in real time, enabling organizations to make decisions based on the most up-to-date information.

### 1. Real-Time Monitoring and Alerts

Stream processing allows businesses to monitor data continuously and trigger alerts when specific conditions are met. For example:

- **Fraud detection** in financial transactions, where real-time monitoring of transaction patterns can detect suspicious activities and flag them immediately.
- **Sensor data monitoring**, where real-time analytics can be used to detect anomalies in manufacturing systems or IoT devices.

## 2. Real-Time Dashboards

Real-time dashboards provide a continuous stream of data that can be analyzed and visualized in real time. These dashboards are commonly used in operational environments where quick action is required based on live data, such as tracking sales performance, website traffic, or inventory levels.

## 3. Data Aggregation and Transformation

Stream processing also enables the aggregation and transformation of data as it flows through the system. This allows businesses to compute real-time metrics, such as average transaction value or click-through rate, and apply transformations to the data, such as filtering or enriching it with additional context.

---

### *Real-World Example: Real-Time Social Media Analytics*

**Real-time social media analytics** is an excellent example of how stream processing is used to gain insights from big data as it's generated. In this scenario, businesses and marketing teams can monitor social media platforms like Twitter, Facebook, and Instagram in real time to understand public sentiment, track brand mentions, and identify emerging trends.

## 1. Data Collection

Social media data is continuously generated in the form of posts, tweets, likes, shares, and comments. Stream processing tools like **Apache Kafka** are used to ingest this data in real time and make it available for analysis.

## 2. Sentiment Analysis

Using tools like **Apache Flink** or **Google Cloud Natural Language API**, businesses can perform sentiment analysis on the social media data to gauge public opinion on a brand, product, or event. This allows companies to react quickly to customer feedback, both positive and negative.

## 3. Trend Detection

By analyzing real-time data streams, businesses can identify trending topics or hashtags as they emerge on social media. This enables companies to participate in conversations while they are still relevant, increasing engagement and visibility.

## 4. Real-Time Reporting

Dashboards displaying real-time social media analytics allow businesses to monitor their online presence and track key metrics such as engagement, reach, and sentiment. These dashboards are often powered by stream processing tools like Flink and Kafka, which provide real-time insights into social media performance.

---

In this chapter, we explored the importance of **real-time data processing** and **streaming analytics** in the modern big data landscape. We discussed the differences between **real-time processing** and **batch processing**, and how tools like **Apache Kafka** and **Apache Flink** enable organizations to process data as it is generated. We also examined how **stream processing** powers real-time applications, such as fraud detection, recommendation engines, and operational monitoring.

Finally, we provided a **real-world example** of **real-time social media analytics**, showcasing how businesses can leverage big data streaming tools to monitor brand sentiment, detect trends, and respond to customer feedback in real time.

As the need for real-time insights continues to grow, stream processing will become even more essential for businesses looking to stay competitive in the fast-paced digital world.

# Chapter 16: The Internet of Things (IoT) and Big Data

The **Internet of Things (IoT)** is rapidly transforming how businesses and consumers interact with technology. With the proliferation of connected devices, sensors, and smart objects, IoT generates vast amounts of data that can be harnessed for valuable insights and decision-making. This chapter will explore how **IoT generates big data**, the processes involved in **processing and analyzing IoT data**, and the **IoT platforms** available for data collection and management. We will conclude with a **real-world example** of how **big data** is applied in **smart homes** to enhance convenience, efficiency, and energy management.

---

### *How IoT Generates Big Data*

The Internet of Things refers to the network of interconnected devices that communicate with each other and with central systems over the internet. IoT devices include everyday objects like **smart thermostats, wearable fitness trackers, connected vehicles, industrial sensors**, and **smart home appliances**. These devices continuously generate massive amounts of data, which is then transmitted to cloud platforms or local storage systems for processing and analysis.

## 1. Data Generation from IoT Devices

Each IoT device collects data from its environment and transmits this information to a central system. Examples of IoT-generated data include:

- **Sensor Data**: Temperature sensors, motion detectors, and humidity sensors collect real-time environmental data.
- **Location Data**: GPS-enabled devices track the location of people, vehicles, or objects.
- **Health Data**: Wearables like fitness trackers collect data on physical activity, heart rate, and sleep patterns.
- **Operational Data**: Industrial machines collect data on performance, usage, and maintenance needs.

The sheer volume of data generated by IoT devices makes it a prime example of **big data**, often characterized by the **3 Vs—volume**, **velocity**, and **variety**:

- **Volume**: The massive amount of data generated by billions of IoT devices.
- **Velocity**: The continuous, real-time flow of data.
- **Variety**: The diverse types of data, including structured, semi-structured, and unstructured data.

## 2. Challenges of IoT Data

The data generated by IoT devices is often unstructured or semi-structured, which can pose challenges for storage and analysis.

Additionally, IoT data tends to be high velocity, with data streams constantly flowing from devices, requiring efficient processing systems to handle this influx of information.

---

## *Processing and Analyzing IoT Data*

IoT data must be processed and analyzed in real time or near real time to derive actionable insights. To effectively manage and analyze IoT data, organizations employ a variety of techniques and tools to handle data at scale.

### 1. Data Processing for IoT

- **Edge Computing**: With edge computing, data is processed closer to where it is generated (at the "edge" of the network) rather than being sent to a central data center. This reduces latency and bandwidth usage while enabling faster decision-making.
    - ○ **Example**: In industrial settings, edge devices can analyze sensor data in real time to identify machine failures and trigger alerts before they cause downtime.
- **Cloud Computing**: Cloud platforms, such as **AWS**, **Microsoft Azure**, and **Google Cloud**, offer scalable storage and computing resources to process and analyze large volumes of IoT data.

o **Example**: Smart homes can use cloud platforms to aggregate data from various devices and apply machine learning algorithms to detect usage patterns and optimize energy consumption.

- **Stream Processing**: Stream processing frameworks, such as **Apache Kafka** and **Apache Flink**, enable real-time analysis of continuous data streams. This is especially useful for time-sensitive applications like monitoring traffic flow or detecting fraudulent activity in financial transactions.

## 2. Data Analysis for IoT

- **Predictive Analytics**: By applying machine learning models to historical IoT data, businesses can predict future events or trends, such as maintenance needs for industrial equipment or customer behavior in smart retail environments.

- **Anomaly Detection**: By continuously monitoring data, organizations can use AI and statistical methods to identify outliers or unusual patterns, which may indicate system failures, security breaches, or abnormal behavior.

- **Visualization**: Visualizing IoT data with dashboards and charts enables decision-makers to easily interpret complex datasets and take action based on real-time insights.

    o **Example**: In smart cities, IoT sensors in traffic lights and vehicles can be visualized on maps to monitor traffic congestion and adjust traffic flow accordingly.

*IoT Platforms for Data Collection and Management*

IoT platforms are specialized systems designed to collect, manage, and process data from a variety of IoT devices. These platforms typically offer integrated tools for device management, data storage, data analytics, and application integration.

## 1. Key Features of IoT Platforms

- **Device Management**: IoT platforms allow businesses to manage large fleets of connected devices, including device provisioning, configuration, monitoring, and maintenance.
- **Data Ingestion**: These platforms provide scalable ways to collect and ingest data from IoT sensors and devices, often through protocols like **MQTT** or **CoAP**.
- **Data Storage**: IoT platforms offer cloud storage or edge storage solutions for storing vast amounts of sensor data. This can include both real-time and historical data.
- **Data Analytics**: IoT platforms often come with built-in analytics tools or integrate with third-party analytics solutions to derive insights from IoT data.
- **Security**: IoT platforms implement security measures such as data encryption, authentication, and access control to protect IoT devices and data.

## 2. Popular IoT Platforms

- **AWS IoT**: Amazon Web Services offers a suite of IoT services, including **AWS IoT Core**, which allows users to securely connect devices, collect and analyze data, and integrate with other AWS services.

- **Microsoft Azure IoT**: Azure IoT Hub and Azure IoT Central provide cloud-based solutions for device management, data collection, and analysis, along with tools for predictive maintenance and real-time monitoring.

- **Google Cloud IoT**: Google Cloud offers IoT services like **Cloud IoT Core**, which helps businesses securely connect and manage devices, as well as tools for integrating IoT data with machine learning models and analytics.

## 3. IoT Protocols

IoT platforms use a variety of protocols for device communication and data exchange. Common IoT protocols include:

- **MQTT (Message Queuing Telemetry Transport)**: A lightweight messaging protocol designed for low-bandwidth, high-latency networks.

- **CoAP (Constrained Application Protocol)**: A protocol optimized for low-power devices with limited processing capabilities.

- **HTTP/HTTPS**: Standard web protocols for communication, often used when IoT devices need to interact with cloud-based services.

## *Real-World Example: Big Data in Smart Homes*

**Smart homes** are a perfect example of how IoT generates big data, and how that data can be processed, analyzed, and acted upon to improve the convenience, efficiency, and security of residential living. In a smart home, IoT devices such as thermostats, lights, door locks, security cameras, and appliances are interconnected and can send data to a central system or cloud platform.

### 1. Data Collection in Smart Homes

Smart homes rely on a variety of sensors and connected devices to collect data about the household's environment:

- **Temperature and Humidity Sensors**: Devices like **Nest Thermostat** or **Ecobee** collect data on indoor climate and can adjust the temperature in real time to optimize energy usage.

- **Motion Sensors**: Devices such as **Ring Doorbell** or **Philips Hue** lights collect data on occupancy and movement within the home to trigger actions like turning on lights or locking doors.

- **Energy Consumption Data**: **Smart plugs** and **smart meters** provide data on energy consumption patterns, enabling homeowners to monitor and reduce their electricity usage.

## 2. Processing and Analyzing Smart Home Data

The data collected by IoT devices is sent to the cloud, where it can be processed and analyzed:

- **Energy Optimization**: By analyzing energy consumption patterns, smart thermostats can predict the best times to adjust temperatures and lower energy bills.
- **Security Monitoring**: Real-time data from cameras and motion sensors is processed to detect unusual activity, alerting homeowners or authorities if necessary.
- **Predictive Maintenance**: IoT-enabled devices like smart refrigerators or washing machines can predict failures by analyzing usage data and alerting homeowners when maintenance is required.

## 3. Smart Home Platforms

Many smart home ecosystems use IoT platforms to manage the connected devices and data:

- **Amazon Alexa**: Provides a cloud platform for integrating various smart home devices and enabling voice commands for controlling devices.
- **Google Home**: Similar to Amazon Alexa, Google Home integrates with IoT devices, providing a central platform for managing smart home operations.

- **Apple HomeKit**: Apple's IoT framework allows devices to be controlled through the Apple ecosystem, integrating smart home features into iPhones, iPads, and Siri.

## 4. Benefits of IoT in Smart Homes

- **Energy Efficiency**: By automating temperature control and lighting, smart homes can significantly reduce energy consumption and costs.
- **Convenience**: Homeowners can remotely monitor and control devices, receiving real-time alerts and insights on their mobile devices.
- **Enhanced Security**: IoT-enabled security systems allow homeowners to monitor their property remotely and respond quickly to potential threats.

---

In this chapter, we explored the relationship between **IoT** and **big data** and how IoT devices generate vast amounts of data that can be processed and analyzed to improve business outcomes and personal convenience. We discussed the importance of **real-time data processing** for analyzing IoT data, and reviewed tools such as **Apache Kafka** and **Apache Flink** that enable real-time stream processing. We also highlighted the role of **IoT platforms** in collecting, managing, and securing IoT data.

Finally, we examined a **real-world example** of how big data is utilized in **smart homes**, where IoT devices collect data to optimize energy consumption, enhance security, and improve the convenience of everyday living.

As IoT continues to evolve, the integration of big data analytics into IoT systems will unlock new possibilities for businesses and consumers alike, enabling smarter, more efficient, and more connected environments.

# Chapter 17: Big Data in the Cloud

Cloud computing has revolutionized how businesses store, process, and analyze big data. With its scalable, flexible, and cost-effective nature, the cloud provides organizations with the ability to handle large datasets without the need for extensive on-premises infrastructure. This chapter will explore **the cloud's role in big data storage and computing**, **cloud data management solutions** for big data, and the **hybrid cloud** and **multi-cloud architectures** that are increasingly being adopted. We will conclude with a **real-world example** of how **big data storage** is leveraged in **video streaming services**.

---

### *The Cloud's Role in Big Data Storage and Computing*

The cloud has become a crucial component of big data strategies because it offers nearly unlimited resources for storage and computing. Traditional on-premises solutions often struggle with the volume, velocity, and variety of big data, whereas the cloud is specifically designed to scale with these demands.

### 1. Scalable Storage Solutions

Big data storage solutions in the cloud are highly scalable, allowing businesses to store massive amounts of data without having to invest in physical hardware. Cloud storage services are designed to grow with your data needs, offering **pay-as-you-go** models where businesses only pay for the storage they use.

- **Object Storage**: Cloud providers offer object storage solutions, such as **Amazon S3**, **Azure Blob Storage**, and **Google Cloud Storage**, which allow businesses to store large, unstructured data (e.g., images, videos, and log files) in a scalable and cost-effective way.

- **Data Lakes**: Cloud-based **data lakes** (e.g., **AWS Lake Formation** and **Azure Data Lake Storage**) are designed for storing vast amounts of raw, unstructured data in its native format, enabling businesses to process and analyze data without having to pre-process it.

## 2. Cloud Computing for Big Data

Cloud computing provides the computing power needed to process big data. Unlike traditional on-premises systems, which can be expensive to scale, cloud platforms offer elastic computing resources that can be dynamically allocated based on demand.

- **Virtual Machines (VMs)**: Cloud providers like **AWS EC2**, **Azure Virtual Machines**, and **Google Compute Engine** allow businesses to run virtual machines with different configurations to process large datasets without the need for physical hardware.

- **Managed Big Data Services**: Cloud providers offer managed services for big data processing, such as **Amazon EMR**, **Google Dataproc**, and **Azure HDInsight**, which allow businesses to use distributed processing frameworks like **Hadoop**, **Spark**, and **Flink** with minimal setup and management overhead.

---

## *Cloud Data Management Solutions for Big Data*

Effective data management is essential for ensuring the integrity, accessibility, and security of big data. Cloud platforms provide a range of services that help businesses manage their data efficiently and securely.

### 1. Data Governance

Data governance refers to the practices, policies, and standards used to manage data within an organization. Cloud platforms offer tools for data governance that ensure compliance, security, and efficient data management:

- **Data Catalogs**: Services like **AWS Glue Data Catalog**, **Google Cloud Data Catalog**, and **Azure Purview** allow businesses to organize and tag data, making it easier to search and access.
- **Metadata Management**: Cloud providers offer metadata management solutions that enable businesses to track the

origins and transformations of their data, helping maintain data quality and consistency.

## 2. Data Security and Compliance

Securing big data is critical to protecting sensitive information and maintaining customer trust. Cloud platforms offer a variety of security features to ensure that data is protected at rest, in transit, and during processing:

- **Encryption**: Cloud providers offer encryption for both **data at rest** (e.g., stored on disks or cloud storage) and **data in transit** (e.g., transmitted over networks), using protocols like **AES** and **SSL/TLS**.
- **Identity and Access Management (IAM)**: Cloud IAM solutions allow businesses to control who can access and modify data. Tools like **AWS IAM, Azure Active Directory**, and **Google Cloud Identity** provide fine-grained access control.
- **Compliance**: Cloud platforms are often compliant with various regulations and standards, such as **GDPR, HIPAA**, and **PCI-DSS**, ensuring that businesses meet the necessary legal and security requirements.

## 3. Data Integration

Cloud platforms facilitate the integration of data from multiple sources, making it easier to create a unified view of the data for analytics:

- **ETL (Extract, Transform, Load)**: Cloud services like **AWS Glue**, **Azure Data Factory**, and **Google Cloud Dataflow** provide managed ETL tools to extract data from various sources, transform it into the right format, and load it into storage systems for further analysis.
- **APIs**: Many cloud platforms support APIs that allow businesses to connect with external data sources, including third-party applications, IoT devices, and social media platforms, enabling seamless data integration.

## Hybrid Cloud and Multi-Cloud Architectures

As organizations become more complex and adopt diverse technologies, **hybrid cloud** and **multi-cloud** architectures are gaining popularity. These architectures combine on-premises, private cloud, and public cloud solutions to optimize data storage, processing, and security.

### 1. Hybrid Cloud

A **hybrid cloud** architecture combines on-premises infrastructure with public and private cloud services, allowing businesses to move workloads between different environments based on cost, performance, and security requirements.

- **Benefits**:
  - **Flexibility**: Businesses can store sensitive data on private clouds or on-premises while leveraging public clouds for less critical workloads and scalability.
  - **Cost Optimization**: Hybrid cloud solutions enable businesses to use public cloud resources for temporary or burst workloads, while maintaining on-premises infrastructure for long-term storage.
  - **Data Sovereignty**: Organizations can ensure that data remains in specific geographic locations, which is important for regulatory compliance.

## 2. Multi-Cloud

A **multi-cloud** strategy involves using multiple public cloud providers (e.g., AWS, Azure, Google Cloud) to avoid vendor lock-in and increase resilience. In a multi-cloud environment, workloads can be distributed across various providers, allowing organizations to take advantage of the best services offered by each platform.

- **Benefits**:
  - **Resilience**: Multi-cloud architectures provide redundancy, ensuring that if one cloud provider

experiences an outage, services can be maintained by switching to another provider.

- o **Avoiding Vendor Lock-In**: Multi-cloud strategies give organizations the freedom to choose the best tools and services available from different providers, avoiding reliance on a single vendor.
- o **Optimized Performance**: Businesses can choose cloud providers based on specific performance requirements, such as geographical location, compute power, and analytics capabilities.

---

## *Real-World Example: Big Data Storage for Video Streaming Services*

Video streaming services, such as **Netflix**, **Hulu**, and **YouTube**, generate massive amounts of data from content consumption, user behavior, and device interactions. Managing and processing this big data is a complex task that involves cloud computing at its core.

### 1. Data Collection and Storage

Video streaming services collect various types of data, including:

- **User Data**: Information on user preferences, viewing history, and interaction with the platform.
- **Video Data**: Data related to video content, including video quality, format, and metadata (e.g., genre, actors).

- **Device Data**: Information on the devices used to stream content, including device types, locations, and network speeds.

This data is stored on **cloud platforms** such as **Amazon S3**, **Google Cloud Storage**, and **Azure Blob Storage**, which offer scalable storage solutions that can handle large volumes of unstructured data.

## 2. Data Processing and Analytics

Once the data is collected and stored, it is processed and analyzed to gain insights into user behavior, optimize content delivery, and improve the user experience:

- **User Analytics**: Video streaming platforms use machine learning models to analyze user data and recommend personalized content based on viewing history and preferences.
- **Content Delivery Optimization**: By analyzing device data, streaming services can optimize video quality and adjust content delivery for users with slower internet connections.

## 3. Cloud Infrastructure and Scalability

Video streaming services rely on **cloud computing** to scale their infrastructure as demand fluctuates:

- **Auto-Scaling**: Cloud platforms automatically scale the computing resources used for video streaming, ensuring that users can access content even during peak usage times (e.g., during new show releases).

- **Edge Computing**: Video streaming services use **CDNs (Content Delivery Networks)** and **edge computing** to cache and deliver content closer to the end-users, reducing latency and improving video streaming performance.

## 4. Real-Time Analytics

In real time, streaming services analyze user behavior to adjust content recommendations, monitor system performance, and identify potential issues:

- **Real-Time Data Processing**: Tools like **Apache Kafka** and **Apache Flink** are used to process user data streams in real time, enabling instant content recommendations and adjustments to the quality of the stream.

In this chapter, we explored **big data in the cloud** and how cloud computing provides scalable, flexible, and cost-effective solutions for storing, processing, and analyzing large datasets. We discussed cloud data management solutions, including data storage, security, governance, and analytics, as well as the benefits of **hybrid cloud** and **multi-cloud architectures**. We also highlighted a **real-world**

**example** of how **video streaming services** leverage cloud platforms to store and manage massive volumes of data, optimize content delivery, and provide personalized recommendations.

As big data continues to grow, cloud computing will remain a key enabler for businesses to harness the power of data, ensuring scalability, performance, and cost-efficiency while providing innovative solutions across industries.

# Chapter 18: Big Data in Artificial Intelligence

**Artificial Intelligence (AI)** is revolutionizing industries by enabling machines to perform tasks that previously required human intelligence. One of the key drivers behind the rapid advancements in AI is **big data**, which provides the vast amounts of information needed to train and improve AI models. In this chapter, we will explore how **AI benefits from big data**, the process of **training AI models** on large datasets, and the role of big data in two prominent areas of AI: **Natural Language Processing (NLP)** and **Computer Vision**. We will conclude with a **real-world example** of how **big data** powers **AI-powered personal assistants**.

---

### *How AI Benefits from Big Data*

AI relies heavily on **big data** to learn, improve, and make predictions or decisions. Large datasets provide the raw material necessary to train and fine-tune AI models, enabling them to understand complex patterns and make accurate predictions.

### 1. Data-Driven Learning

AI algorithms, particularly those in machine learning and deep learning, learn by analyzing large amounts of data. By training on vast datasets, AI models can:

- **Identify Patterns**: Big data allows AI to detect patterns that may not be apparent in smaller datasets. For example, machine learning algorithms can uncover correlations between variables or recognize trends in customer behavior.
- **Improve Accuracy**: The more data an AI model is exposed to, the better it can refine its predictions and decision-making capabilities. Large datasets help reduce bias and variance, leading to more accurate and reliable models.
- **Generalize to New Data**: By learning from diverse datasets, AI models become better at generalizing their knowledge to new, unseen data, which is essential for real-world applications.

## 2. Enabling Complex AI Applications

Big data is essential for enabling AI applications in complex domains, such as healthcare, finance, and autonomous vehicles. These applications require massive amounts of data to train AI models to make accurate decisions and predictions.

- **Healthcare**: AI models trained on large datasets of medical records, images, and sensor data can assist in diagnosing diseases and predicting treatment outcomes.
- **Finance**: Big data allows AI systems to analyze financial transactions, detect fraud, and optimize trading strategies.

- **Autonomous Vehicles**: Self-driving cars rely on big data from sensors, cameras, and real-time maps to make decisions about navigation and safety.

### 3. Real-Time Insights

AI systems can also leverage big data in real-time to provide instantaneous insights and actions. For example, AI-powered recommendation engines analyze user behavior data in real-time to suggest products or content based on current actions, improving the customer experience.

---

## *Training AI Models on Large Datasets*

Training AI models requires large, high-quality datasets to ensure that the models are accurate, robust, and capable of handling real-world scenarios. The process of training involves feeding data into an AI model, allowing it to learn patterns and make predictions.

### 1. Data Preprocessing

Before training an AI model, the raw data typically needs to be cleaned, transformed, and formatted. This process, known as **data preprocessing**, involves:

- **Handling Missing Data**: Missing values are filled in or removed to avoid bias in the model.

- **Normalization and Standardization**: Features are scaled to similar ranges to ensure that the model treats them equally.
- **Feature Engineering**: New features may be created to improve the model's performance, such as transforming categorical variables into numerical representations.

## 2. Model Training

Once the data is preprocessed, it is fed into machine learning or deep learning models, which are trained to learn from the data. There are two common types of training methods:

- **Supervised Learning**: In supervised learning, the model is trained on labeled data, where both the input data and the correct output (label) are provided. The model learns to map inputs to outputs and generalizes to new data.
- **Unsupervised Learning**: In unsupervised learning, the model is trained on unlabeled data and must find patterns or groupings in the data. This is typically used for clustering, anomaly detection, and dimensionality reduction.

## 3. Model Evaluation and Tuning

After training, AI models are evaluated to ensure they perform well on new, unseen data. Key evaluation metrics include:

- **Accuracy**: The percentage of correct predictions made by the model.

- **Precision and Recall**: Used for classification problems to measure the relevance and completeness of predictions.

- **Loss Functions**: Measures the difference between predicted and actual outcomes, used to optimize the model during training. Once the model is evaluated, hyperparameter tuning is performed to improve its performance. This involves adjusting settings such as the learning rate, number of layers (in deep learning), and regularization techniques.

## Big Data in Natural Language Processing (NLP) and Computer Vision

Two of the most exciting areas of AI are **Natural Language Processing (NLP)** and **Computer Vision**, both of which rely heavily on big data for training models and making accurate predictions.

### 1. Big Data in Natural Language Processing (NLP)

Natural Language Processing (NLP) involves enabling machines to understand, interpret, and generate human language. NLP applications include machine translation, sentiment analysis, and chatbots.

- **Training NLP Models with Big Data**: NLP models are trained on massive text corpora, which may include books, articles, social media posts, and conversations. For example, large datasets like **Wikipedia**, **Common Crawl**, and **social media conversations** are used to train models such as **GPT-3**.

- **Word Embeddings**: NLP models use techniques like **word embeddings** (e.g., **Word2Vec**, **GloVe**) to represent words as vectors in a high-dimensional space, enabling models to capture semantic meaning and relationships between words.

- **Applications**:
  - **Sentiment Analysis**: Analyzing social media posts or customer reviews to gauge public sentiment toward a product or brand.
  - **Language Translation**: Machine translation systems like Google Translate rely on large parallel corpora (text in multiple languages) to train their models.
  - **Chatbots**: AI-powered personal assistants like **Siri** or **Google Assistant** rely on NLP models to understand and respond to user queries.

## 2. Big Data in Computer Vision

Computer vision enables machines to interpret and understand visual information from the world, such as images or videos. Applications of computer vision include facial recognition, image classification, and object detection.

- **Training Computer Vision Models with Big Data**: Computer vision models are trained on massive datasets of labeled images and videos. These datasets may include millions of images, such as **ImageNet**, which contains millions of labeled images across thousands of categories.
- **Convolutional Neural Networks (CNNs)**: CNNs are deep learning models specifically designed for image processing. They are trained on large datasets to automatically detect features in images, such as edges, textures, and patterns.
- **Applications**:
  o **Face Recognition**: AI systems can identify individuals by analyzing facial features in images or video.
  o **Medical Imaging**: AI models trained on large datasets of medical images (e.g., X-rays, MRIs) can assist doctors in diagnosing diseases and detecting anomalies.
  o **Autonomous Vehicles**: Self-driving cars use computer vision to interpret sensor data and navigate the environment.

*Real-World Example: Big Data in AI-Powered Personal Assistants*

**AI-powered personal assistants**, such as **Apple's Siri**, **Amazon's Alexa**, **Google Assistant**, and **Microsoft's Cortana**, rely on big data and AI to understand user queries and provide personalized responses. These personal assistants use a combination of **Natural Language Processing (NLP)** and **machine learning** to interact with users in a natural, conversational way.

## 1. Data Collection

Personal assistants collect data from various sources, including:

- **Voice Commands**: Users interact with personal assistants by speaking commands or asking questions.
- **User Profiles**: Personal assistants learn about the user's preferences, habits, and daily routines, enabling them to provide personalized responses (e.g., reminders, recommendations).
- **External Data Sources**: Personal assistants also gather information from the internet, including weather forecasts, traffic reports, news updates, and more.

## 2. Training AI Models

Personal assistants use big data to train AI models that process and understand natural language:

- **Speech Recognition**: Personal assistants use speech-to-text algorithms to transcribe voice commands into text, which is then analyzed by NLP models.

- **Intent Recognition**: NLP models are trained to understand the user's intent (e.g., setting an alarm, asking for weather information) and respond appropriately.
- **Contextual Understanding**: Over time, personal assistants learn to understand the context of the user's queries based on previous interactions, improving the accuracy and relevance of responses.

## 3. Real-Time Data Processing

AI-powered personal assistants process user queries in real time. They analyze voice inputs, identify intent, and access external data sources to generate relevant responses:

- **Query Processing**: Once the user's voice is converted into text, the personal assistant uses machine learning algorithms to parse the query, understand the context, and generate an appropriate response.
- **Action Execution**: The assistant then takes actions based on the recognized intent, such as sending a text message, setting a reminder, or playing music.

## 4. Benefits

- **Convenience**: Personal assistants automate tasks and provide real-time information, enhancing convenience for users.

- **Personalization**: Through machine learning, personal assistants become more attuned to individual preferences, providing more relevant and personalized responses.
- **Efficiency**: By leveraging big data, AI-powered assistants optimize their interactions, providing faster and more accurate results as they continue to learn from user interactions.

In this chapter, we examined how **big data** is essential to the development and effectiveness of **artificial intelligence**. We explored how AI benefits from big data through improved learning, accurate predictions, and the ability to handle complex tasks. We discussed how **training AI models** on large datasets is critical to creating robust, scalable AI systems and how **big data** is applied in **Natural Language Processing (NLP)** and **Computer Vision** to enable intelligent applications.

Finally, we provided a **real-world example** of how **AI-powered personal assistants** rely on big data to understand user queries, personalize responses, and optimize interactions. As AI continues to evolve, the relationship between big data and AI will only become more critical in driving innovation and enhancing the user experience across various industries.

# Chapter 19: Big Data for Business Intelligence

In today's data-driven world, businesses rely heavily on data to make informed decisions, optimize operations, and maintain a competitive edge. **Business Intelligence (BI)** uses **big data** to transform raw data into actionable insights. This chapter will explore how **big data** supports **decision-making**, review key **BI tools** such as **Power BI**, **Qlik**, and **Tableau**, discuss the integration of **big data** into **advanced BI** applications, and conclude with a **real-world example** of **big data** in **retail** for **customer segmentation**.

---

## *Leveraging Big Data for Decision-Making*

The ability to make data-driven decisions is critical to success in today's business environment. **Big data** provides organizations with vast amounts of information that, when analyzed correctly, can drive smarter decisions.

### 1. Big Data and Decision-Making

Big data empowers decision-makers by offering detailed insights that help organizations:

- **Identify trends and patterns**: Big data enables businesses to detect trends in customer behavior, market conditions, and operational performance. This helps managers make proactive decisions rather than reactive ones.

- **Optimize operations**: Big data allows businesses to optimize various aspects of operations, including supply chain management, inventory control, and resource allocation, leading to cost savings and greater efficiency.
- **Predict future outcomes**: By analyzing historical data, businesses can forecast future trends, allowing them to plan strategically. Predictive analytics enables businesses to anticipate demand, customer preferences, and potential risks.

## 2. The Role of Data in Decision-Making

- **Data-Driven Culture**: Businesses that embrace a **data-driven culture** ensure that decision-making is based on evidence and insights derived from data rather than intuition or guesswork.
- **Real-Time Insights**: Real-time data processing and analytics enable decision-makers to respond quickly to emerging trends or issues, such as market shifts, customer feedback, or operational disruptions.

## 3. Business Value of Big Data

By leveraging big data for decision-making, businesses can:

- **Enhance customer experience**: Personalizing interactions and recommendations based on real-time data insights.

- **Improve financial performance**: Making more accurate financial predictions and optimizing resource allocation to increase profitability.

- **Gain a competitive edge**: Using data to uncover new opportunities, identify market gaps, and stay ahead of competitors.

---

## *Tools for Business Intelligence: Power BI, Qlik, Tableau*

There are several powerful tools available that help organizations turn big data into actionable insights. Some of the leading **Business Intelligence (BI) tools** are **Power BI**, **Qlik**, and **Tableau**, each with its unique features, strengths, and use cases.

### 1. Power BI

**Microsoft Power BI** is a widely used BI tool that allows businesses to create interactive visualizations and business intelligence dashboards.

- **Key Features**:
    - **Data Connectivity**: Power BI supports integration with a wide variety of data sources, including SQL databases, Excel files, and cloud services like Azure and Google Analytics.
    - **Interactive Dashboards**: Users can create dynamic dashboards with drag-and-drop functionality to

visualize key metrics, such as sales performance, marketing campaigns, and customer behavior.

- o **Natural Language Query**: Power BI allows users to query their data in natural language, simplifying data analysis for non-technical users.

- **Strengths**:
  - o Seamless integration with Microsoft Office tools.
  - o Affordable and easy to use for businesses of all sizes.
  - o Strong support for cloud-based data analytics and collaboration.

## 2. Qlik

**Qlik** is another popular BI tool known for its associative data model, which allows users to explore data from multiple angles and uncover hidden insights.

- **Key Features**:
  - o **Qlik Sense**: A self-service BI tool that enables users to create interactive reports and dashboards with advanced visualizations.
  - o **Data Integration**: Qlik can integrate data from multiple sources, including databases, spreadsheets, and cloud applications, providing a unified view of business performance.

- **Associative Model**: Qlik's associative model allows users to explore data freely by making selections and exploring associations between different data points.
- **Strengths**:
  - Excellent for in-depth data exploration and uncovering insights that might not be obvious.
  - Scalable for both small businesses and large enterprises.
  - Strong support for mobile BI.

## 3. Tableau

**Tableau** is known for its powerful data visualization capabilities and is widely used to create interactive, easy-to-understand dashboards and reports.

- **Key Features**:
  - **Data Connectivity**: Tableau integrates with a variety of data sources, including relational databases, cloud platforms, and Excel files.
  - **Visualization**: Tableau offers a wide range of chart types, including bar charts, pie charts, heatmaps, and geographic maps, which can be customized for different types of data.
  - **Drag-and-Drop Interface**: Tableau's user-friendly interface allows users to quickly build complex visualizations without needing to write code.

- **Strengths**:
  - Highly intuitive and easy for non-technical users to pick up.
  - Excellent for creating visually appealing and interactive dashboards.
  - Strong community support and rich resources for training.

---

## *Advanced BI with Big Data Integration*

With the rise of big data, traditional BI tools have evolved to handle the volume, velocity, and variety of modern datasets. Integrating big data into BI systems is crucial for gaining deeper insights and driving smarter decision-making.

### 1. Integrating Big Data with BI Tools

- **Data Warehouses**: Big data from various sources is aggregated in **data warehouses** like **Amazon Redshift**, **Google BigQuery**, and **Azure Synapse**, where it is cleaned, transformed, and made available for analysis.
- **Cloud BI Solutions**: Many BI tools are now integrated with cloud platforms, allowing businesses to store and process big data more easily. **Power BI**, **Tableau**, and **Qlik** all support cloud data sources and can scale with the growing volume of big data.

- **Real-Time Analytics**: With the advent of real-time data processing frameworks like **Apache Kafka** and **Apache Flink**, BI tools can now analyze data as it is generated, providing near-instant insights for decision-makers.

## 2. Data Visualization for Big Data

The challenge of visualizing big data lies in presenting vast amounts of information in a way that is easy to understand. BI tools like Tableau, Qlik, and Power BI allow businesses to:

- **Create dashboards** that aggregate and display data in real-time.

- **Use interactive features** like drill-downs, filters, and dynamic charts to enable users to explore data in-depth.

- **Present trends and patterns** through visual means such as heatmaps, scatter plots, and geographical maps, making it easier to spot key insights at a glance.

## 3. Predictive and Prescriptive Analytics

Advanced BI systems with big data integration can go beyond descriptive analytics and provide **predictive** and **prescriptive analytics**:

- **Predictive Analytics**: By analyzing historical data, BI tools can predict future trends and outcomes (e.g., sales forecasts, demand predictions).

- **Prescriptive Analytics**: BI systems can recommend actions to optimize business performance, such as adjusting marketing campaigns or inventory management strategies.

---

*Real-World Example: Big Data in Retail (Customer Segmentation)*
Customer segmentation is a common application of **big data** and **business intelligence** in the retail industry. Retailers collect vast amounts of data from various sources, including in-store purchases, online transactions, social media interactions, and customer feedback. This data is then analyzed and segmented to create targeted marketing campaigns, improve product offerings, and optimize customer experiences.

## 1. Data Collection for Customer Segmentation
Retailers gather customer data from a variety of touchpoints:

- **Point-of-Sale (POS) Data**: Transaction data from in-store purchases.
- **Online Behavior**: Data from e-commerce sites, including browsing history, cart activity, and purchase history.
- **Social Media**: Customer interactions on platforms like Facebook, Twitter, and Instagram.
- **Customer Feedback**: Surveys, reviews, and customer service interactions provide insights into customer satisfaction and preferences.

## 2. Data Analysis for Segmentation

By integrating big data from these sources, retailers can use **business intelligence tools** to analyze customer behavior and segment their audience based on different factors:

- **Demographic Segmentation**: Grouping customers by age, gender, income level, or geographic location.
- **Behavioral Segmentation**: Segmenting customers based on purchasing behavior, such as frequent buyers, occasional shoppers, and seasonal buyers.
- **Psychographic Segmentation**: Segmenting customers based on their interests, values, and lifestyle choices, which can be derived from social media and feedback data.

## 3. Creating Targeted Marketing Campaigns

Once the customer segments are identified, retailers can use the insights to create personalized marketing strategies:

- **Tailored Promotions**: Offering personalized discounts or product recommendations based on customer behavior and preferences.
- **Email Campaigns**: Sending targeted emails with product recommendations, discounts, or exclusive offers tailored to individual customer segments.
- **Product Development**: Identifying which customer segments are most interested in certain product types,

enabling retailers to adjust their inventory and marketing strategies.

## 4. Outcome

By leveraging **big data** and **business intelligence** tools, retailers can improve customer satisfaction, increase sales, and build long-lasting customer relationships. The ability to analyze and segment customers based on big data allows businesses to deliver more relevant and effective marketing campaigns, enhancing their competitive advantage in the retail space.

---

In this chapter, we explored how **big data** plays a critical role in **business intelligence**, enabling organizations to make data-driven decisions that optimize performance, reduce costs, and improve customer experiences. We discussed the **BI tools** available for analyzing big data, such as **Power BI**, **Qlik**, and **Tableau**, and how these tools integrate with big data for advanced analytics. We also examined the application of **big data** in **retail** for **customer segmentation**, showcasing how organizations can leverage big data to understand their customers better and create targeted marketing strategies.

As businesses continue to generate and collect more data, the role of **business intelligence** and **big data analytics** will only grow, driving smarter decision-making and more personalized experiences across industries.

# Chapter 20: Ethics and Bias in Big Data

As big data continues to shape industries and drive innovation, it also brings forth significant ethical considerations. The collection and use of vast amounts of data raise questions about privacy, fairness, accountability, and the potential for bias in AI and machine learning models. In this chapter, we will explore the **ethical implications** of big data collection and use, discuss how to **detect and address bias** in big data models, and highlight the importance of **ensuring fairness** in AI and big data applications. We will conclude with a **real-world example** of **bias in hiring algorithms**.

---

### *The Ethical Implications of Big Data Collection and Use*

The vast quantities of data collected by organizations raise several ethical concerns, particularly around privacy, consent, and the potential misuse of information. As businesses increasingly rely on big data to drive decision-making, it is important to consider the ethical implications of collecting and using this data.

### 1. Privacy Concerns

With the growing reliance on big data, businesses often collect sensitive personal information from individuals, such as location data, browsing history, and social media activity. The ethical question arises when this data is used without informed consent or when it is used in ways that individuals did not anticipate. For instance:

- **Data Breaches**: Personal data can be exposed in the event of a cyberattack or data breach, leading to privacy violations.
- **Surveillance**: Data collection can sometimes be used for invasive surveillance, which raises questions about individuals' right to privacy.
- **Solutions**:
  - o **Informed Consent**: Organizations must ensure that data collection practices are transparent and that individuals understand what data is being collected and how it will be used.
  - o **Data Minimization**: Collect only the data necessary for the task at hand, reducing the potential for misuse.
  - o **Anonymization**: Ensure that personally identifiable information (PII) is anonymized or pseudonymized to protect individuals' identities.

## 2. Ownership of Data

Another ethical issue is the ownership of data. Who owns the data collected by businesses, and who has the right to access it? In many cases, individuals may not be aware that their personal data is being collected, leading to questions about the **ownership** and **control** of that data. For example:

- **Third-Party Data Sharing**: Companies may share or sell customer data to third parties without fully informing the individuals whose data is being sold.
- **Data Usage**: Data collected for one purpose (e.g., improving customer service) may later be used for a completely different purpose (e.g., targeted advertising).
- **Solutions**:
  - **Clear Privacy Policies**: Organizations should provide clear and transparent privacy policies that outline data ownership, access, and usage.
  - **User Control**: Provide individuals with the ability to control their data, including opting out of data collection or deleting their data entirely.

## 3. Accountability and Transparency

As organizations use AI and machine learning models that rely on big data, it is essential to ensure **accountability** and **transparency** in how data is used to make decisions. If an algorithm makes a decision, who is responsible for that decision? Can the reasoning behind the algorithm be explained? Without transparency, it is difficult to assess whether data-driven decisions are fair and ethical.

- **Solutions**:
  - **Explainable AI (XAI)**: Use machine learning models that offer interpretability, allowing decision-

makers to understand how and why a model arrived at a particular decision.

○ **Auditing and Oversight**: Implement regular audits of algorithms and data use to ensure they align with ethical standards.

---

### Detecting and Addressing Bias in Big Data Models

Bias is one of the most significant challenges in big data analytics and AI. If big data models are trained on biased data, they will likely produce biased results, perpetuating inequality and discrimination. Detecting and addressing bias in big data models is essential to ensure fair and equitable outcomes.

#### 1. Sources of Bias

Bias can enter big data models in various ways:

• **Bias in Data**: If the data used to train models reflects historical biases or stereotypes, the model will inherit these biases. For example, if historical hiring data reflects discrimination against a certain gender or ethnicity, the model trained on that data may continue to favor those groups.

• **Bias in Algorithms**: Algorithms themselves can introduce bias if they are designed in ways that favor certain groups over others. For example, an algorithm used to predict creditworthiness may be biased if it relies too heavily on factors that correlate with race or socioeconomic status.

- **Data Collection Bias**: Bias can also occur in the data collection process, where certain groups are underrepresented or misrepresented in the data, leading to inaccurate or unfair outcomes.

## 2. Methods to Detect Bias

Detecting bias requires a systematic approach to evaluating both the data and the models:

- **Bias Detection Tools**: Use tools and techniques, such as **Fairness Indicators** and **AI Fairness 360**, to assess the fairness of data and models.
- **Bias Audits**: Conduct regular audits to evaluate whether the data and algorithms are fair and do not disadvantage certain groups.
- **Statistical Tests**: Perform statistical tests to identify disparities in how different demographic groups are treated by the model.

## 3. Addressing Bias

Once bias is detected, it is essential to take steps to mitigate it:

- **Bias Mitigation in Data**: Use techniques such as **re-sampling**, **re-weighting**, or **data augmentation** to balance underrepresented groups and reduce bias in the dataset.

- **Algorithmic Fairness**: Modify algorithms to ensure that they do not unfairly discriminate against certain groups. This may involve adjusting decision thresholds or incorporating fairness constraints into the model.

- **Bias in Decision-Making**: Implement **human oversight** to evaluate model outcomes and ensure that they align with ethical standards before they are applied in real-world decisions.

---

### *Ensuring Fairness in AI and Big Data Applications*

Ensuring fairness is crucial to preventing discrimination and promoting equity in AI and big data applications. Fairness in AI refers to the idea that algorithms and data-driven decisions should treat all individuals and groups equitably, without favoring one over another.

### 1. Defining Fairness

Fairness can be difficult to define, as it may mean different things in different contexts. For example:

- **Group Fairness**: Ensures that different demographic groups (e.g., race, gender, age) are treated equally in terms of outcomes.

- **Individual Fairness**: Ensures that similar individuals are treated similarly by the model, regardless of their group affiliation.

## 2. Fairness Techniques

Several techniques can be used to ensure fairness in AI and big data applications:

- **Fairness Constraints**: Integrating fairness constraints into the model training process to ensure that the model does not discriminate against any group.
- **Debiasing Algorithms**: Using algorithms designed to reduce bias, such as adversarial debiasing or fairness regularization.
- **Auditing for Fairness**: Continuously monitor the model's performance across different demographic groups to identify and address any fairness issues.

## 3. Ethical AI Frameworks

Organizations can adopt ethical AI frameworks to guide their development and implementation of AI models. These frameworks often include principles such as **transparency**, **accountability**, **privacy**, and **fairness**, ensuring that AI applications are developed and deployed ethically.

## *Real-World Example: Bias in Hiring Algorithms*

One of the most discussed real-world examples of bias in AI and big data applications is in **hiring algorithms**. Many companies use AI-powered recruitment tools to screen resumes, assess candidates, and even conduct interviews. However, if these algorithms are trained on biased data, they can perpetuate existing discrimination, favoring certain candidates over others based on gender, ethnicity, or age.

### 1. Problem of Bias in Hiring Algorithms

- **Historical Bias**: If an AI recruitment system is trained on historical hiring data, it may inherit biases present in past hiring practices. For example, if the company has historically hired more men than women for technical roles, the algorithm may favor male candidates, even if unintentionally.

- **Data Representation**: If the training data used to build the algorithm is not representative of diverse candidates, the algorithm may be biased toward certain groups, such as those with more traditional education or work experience, disadvantaging others.

### 2. Addressing Bias in Hiring Algorithms

- **Diversifying the Data**: Ensure that the data used to train hiring algorithms is diverse and representative of the candidate pool. This could involve sourcing data from a wider range of backgrounds, education levels, and career experiences.

- **Bias Audits**: Conduct regular audits of the hiring algorithm to evaluate its fairness and detect any potential biases in its recommendations or decisions.

- **Transparent Models**: Use explainable AI models to ensure that the reasoning behind hiring decisions can be understood and audited, allowing organizations to identify any sources of bias.

## 3. Outcome

Addressing bias in hiring algorithms is crucial for ensuring that hiring decisions are fair and equitable. By identifying and mitigating bias, companies can promote diversity, inclusion, and fairness in their recruitment processes.

In this chapter, we explored the **ethical implications** of big data collection and use, emphasizing the importance of privacy, transparency, and accountability in handling sensitive information. We discussed how bias can enter big data models and the methods available to **detect and address bias**, ensuring that AI systems are fair and equitable. Finally, we examined a **real-world example** of **bias in hiring algorithms**, illustrating the potential harm caused by biased AI systems and the steps that can be taken to mitigate such issues.

As the use of big data and AI continues to expand, organizations must prioritize **ethics** and **fairness** in their data practices, ensuring that they use technology to benefit all individuals equitably and responsibly.

# Chapter 21: The Future of Big Data

Big data is an ever-evolving field, driven by rapid advancements in technology. As the volume, velocity, and variety of data continue to grow, new innovations and trends are shaping the future of how we store, process, and analyze data. In this chapter, we will explore **emerging trends** in big data, including the impact of **quantum computing**, **AI**, and **automation**. We will also discuss the rise of **edge computing** for big data and explore how big data intersects with **sustainability** and environmental considerations. Finally, we will look at a **real-world example** of how **big data** is transforming the healthcare industry.

---

### *Emerging Trends in Big Data: Quantum Computing, AI, and Automation*

The future of big data is closely tied to the rapid advancements in various technological fields. **Quantum computing**, **artificial intelligence (AI)**, and **automation** are among the most promising trends, offering transformative potential for how data is processed, analyzed, and used.

#### 1. Quantum Computing and Big Data

**Quantum computing** has the potential to revolutionize the way big data is handled. Unlike classical computers, which rely on bits to represent data as 0s and 1s, quantum computers use **qubits** that can exist in multiple states simultaneously. This allows quantum computers to process massive amounts of data much faster and more efficiently than current technologies.

- **Impact on Big Data**:
    - **Speed**: Quantum computing could dramatically reduce the time required to solve complex problems, such as data encryption, optimization, and simulation tasks. This is especially important for applications involving large-scale datasets, such as climate modeling and financial forecasting.
    - **Optimization**: Quantum algorithms could be used to solve optimization problems that are difficult for classical computers, like supply chain optimization, traffic management, and resource allocation.
    - **Data Security**: Quantum computing could introduce new encryption methods that are more secure than current algorithms, providing enhanced protection for sensitive data.

However, quantum computing is still in its early stages, and it will likely take years before it can be fully integrated into big data systems.

## 2. AI and Automation in Big Data

**Artificial Intelligence (AI)** and **machine learning** are already playing a critical role in big data analytics by helping businesses extract insights from complex datasets. As AI technology advances, it will continue to automate the process of data analysis, making it more efficient and accessible.

- **Automated Data Analytics**: AI can automate data preprocessing, feature extraction, and even model selection, reducing the need for manual intervention and speeding up the data analysis process.
- **Predictive Analytics**: Machine learning algorithms can be used to analyze historical big data and predict future trends, enabling businesses to make data-driven decisions based on forecasts rather than relying solely on historical data.
- **Data Integration**: AI systems can help integrate data from multiple sources, providing a unified view of complex datasets and enabling businesses to gain a more comprehensive understanding of their operations.

With **automation** and **AI** working together, data scientists and analysts will be able to focus more on interpreting results and making strategic decisions rather than spending time on data cleaning and analysis.

*The Rise of Edge Computing for Big Data*

**Edge computing** is another emerging trend in big data that is closely tied to the increasing number of IoT devices and the need for real-time data processing. Edge computing involves processing data closer to the source of generation (e.g., IoT devices, sensors) rather than sending all the data to centralized cloud servers for analysis.

## 1. Benefits of Edge Computing for Big Data

- **Reduced Latency**: By processing data locally, edge computing minimizes the delay between data collection and action, which is critical for real-time applications like autonomous vehicles, industrial automation, and smart cities.

- **Bandwidth Efficiency**: Rather than sending large amounts of raw data to the cloud, edge computing allows for local filtering and processing of data, reducing the strain on network bandwidth and cutting down on data transmission costs.

- **Enhanced Security**: Edge computing can improve data security by keeping sensitive data closer to its source, reducing the risks associated with transmitting data over long distances.

## 2. Applications of Edge Computing in Big Data

- **IoT Devices**: In smart homes, smart cities, and industrial environments, edge computing allows IoT devices to process data locally, enabling quicker responses and better management of resources.

- **Autonomous Vehicles**: Self-driving cars rely on edge computing to process sensor data (e.g., camera feeds, radar) in real time, allowing them to make immediate decisions, such as avoiding obstacles or adjusting speed.
- **Healthcare**: Edge computing can be used in medical devices that monitor patient vital signs. By processing data at the point of collection, edge devices can immediately alert healthcare professionals if any critical conditions are detected.

As the number of connected devices increases, edge computing will become increasingly vital for handling and processing the huge volumes of data generated.

---

### *Big Data and Sustainability: Environmental Considerations*

As the volume of data grows, so does the environmental impact of storing, processing, and managing this data. The energy consumption required for big data operations—particularly in data centers—has raised concerns about the carbon footprint of these activities.

### 1. Energy Consumption in Data Centers

Data centers, which house the hardware required to store and process big data, are responsible for a significant portion of global energy consumption. The need for cooling, along with the power requirements of servers and storage devices, contributes to this energy usage.

- **Green Data Centers**: In response to environmental concerns, there is a growing trend toward building energy-efficient, **green data centers** that utilize renewable energy sources, like solar and wind, to power operations.
- **Energy-Efficient Hardware**: Advances in hardware design, such as low-power processors and energy-efficient storage systems, can help reduce the carbon footprint of big data operations.
- **Data Minimization**: Reducing the amount of data stored and processed can also help mitigate environmental impact. This includes eliminating redundant data, compressing datasets, and adopting techniques like **data deduplication**.

## 2. Sustainability in Big Data Analytics

Big data also has the potential to help promote sustainability in other sectors:

- **Climate Change Research**: Big data analytics can be used to model climate change, predict its effects, and optimize resource use to reduce environmental impact.

- **Smart Cities**: Data collected from IoT devices in smart cities can help reduce energy consumption by optimizing traffic flow, reducing waste, and improving the management of resources like water and electricity.

- **Agriculture**: Big data in agriculture can be used to optimize crop production, reduce water usage, and minimize the use of pesticides, contributing to more sustainable farming practices.

While big data and cloud computing have environmental implications, they also provide the tools to address and mitigate these challenges, enabling smarter and more sustainable practices across industries.

---

### *Real-World Example: Predicting the Future of Big Data in Healthcare*

The healthcare industry is one of the most promising fields for big data applications, where the combination of **electronic health records (EHRs)**, **wearable devices**, and **medical imaging** creates massive datasets that can be analyzed to improve patient outcomes, reduce costs, and optimize care delivery.

### 1. Big Data in Healthcare

- **Data Collection**: Healthcare generates vast amounts of data, including patient demographics, medical histories, lab results, imaging data, and wearable device readings. This data is increasingly being digitized and stored in electronic systems, enabling more efficient data collection and retrieval.

- **Data Integration**: Big data tools help integrate data from various sources, creating a unified view of patient health that can be used for more accurate diagnoses and treatment plans.

- **Predictive Analytics**: By analyzing historical healthcare data, predictive models can forecast disease outbreaks, patient readmissions, and even individual patient health risks. For instance, predictive analytics can be used to identify patients at risk of developing chronic conditions like diabetes, enabling early intervention.

## 2. The Future of Big Data in Healthcare

- **AI and Machine Learning**: The integration of **AI** and **machine learning** with big data in healthcare will enable more personalized medicine, where treatments are tailored to the individual based on their unique health data and genetic makeup.

- **Telemedicine**: The rise of telemedicine will generate additional streams of healthcare data, which can be used to improve virtual care delivery and monitor patient progress remotely.

- **Real-Time Health Monitoring**: Wearable devices will continue to provide real-time health data, which can be analyzed using big data tools to alert healthcare providers about potential issues before they become critical.

By leveraging big data, healthcare systems can become more proactive rather than reactive, improving patient outcomes while reducing costs and inefficiencies.

---

In this chapter, we explored **emerging trends** in big data, including the transformative impact of **quantum computing**, **AI**, and **automation**. We also discussed the rise of **edge computing** and its role in real-time data processing, as well as the environmental considerations associated with big data operations. Finally, we examined a **real-world example** of how big data is revolutionizing the healthcare industry, providing personalized treatments, improving patient care, and predicting future health trends.

The future of big data is rich with possibilities, from harnessing the power of AI to integrating sustainability practices in data centers. As technologies continue to evolve, the potential for big data to solve complex problems and drive innovation will only continue to grow.

# Chapter 22: Big Data in Action

Big data has become an integral part of various industries, transforming how businesses operate, make decisions, and interact with customers. Its applications are vast, ranging from improving healthcare outcomes to optimizing supply chains and enabling personalized marketing. In this chapter, we will explore **real-world applications** of big data across several industries, delve into **case studies** in **healthcare, finance**, and **e-commerce**, and examine the **impact of big data** on **society** and the **economy**. Finally, we will conclude with a **real-world example** of how big data is applied in **smart agriculture**.

---

### *Real-World Applications of Big Data Across Industries*

Big data is revolutionizing industries by providing deeper insights, enabling predictive analytics, and optimizing operational efficiency. Below are some of the key industries where big data is having a transformative impact:

### 1. Healthcare

In the healthcare industry, big data allows for the aggregation of patient records, diagnostic imaging, sensor data, and genomics information to improve patient care and reduce costs.

- **Personalized Medicine**: Big data helps tailor treatments to individual patients based on their genetic makeup, health history, and real-time health data.

- **Predictive Analytics**: Big data tools can predict disease outbreaks, patient readmissions, and potential health risks, allowing for early intervention and better resource allocation.

- **Clinical Research**: Analyzing vast datasets from clinical trials and medical studies can speed up the development of new treatments and pharmaceuticals.

## 2. Finance

The financial sector uses big data to detect fraud, optimize trading strategies, manage risk, and offer personalized financial services to customers.

- **Fraud Detection**: Real-time transaction data is analyzed using machine learning models to identify fraudulent activity, reducing financial losses and protecting customer assets.

- **Algorithmic Trading**: Big data and AI are used in algorithmic trading to analyze market conditions, predict price movements, and execute high-frequency trades with speed and precision.

- **Credit Scoring**: Big data allows for a more accurate assessment of an individual's creditworthiness by incorporating non-traditional data sources, such as social media activity and payment history.

## 3. E-Commerce

In e-commerce, big data plays a crucial role in enhancing the customer experience, optimizing supply chains, and personalizing marketing efforts.

- **Personalized Recommendations**: Online retailers like Amazon use big data to analyze customer behavior and preferences, delivering personalized product recommendations and improving customer engagement.
- **Supply Chain Optimization**: Big data enables e-commerce businesses to optimize inventory management, track shipments, and predict demand trends to minimize stockouts and overstock situations.
- **Customer Sentiment Analysis**: E-commerce companies analyze social media, product reviews, and customer feedback to understand customer sentiment and improve products and services.

## 4. Manufacturing and Supply Chain

Big data helps manufacturers optimize production processes, predict maintenance, and manage the flow of materials in supply chains.

- **Predictive Maintenance**: IoT sensors on equipment generate data that can be analyzed to predict when machinery will fail, reducing downtime and maintenance costs.

- **Supply Chain Optimization**: Big data helps in the management of global supply chains by analyzing inventory levels, supplier performance, and market demand to ensure timely production and distribution.

## 5. Transportation and Logistics

Big data is used to optimize routes, reduce fuel consumption, and manage fleet performance in the transportation and logistics industry.

- **Route Optimization**: Traffic data, weather patterns, and historical driving data are analyzed to optimize delivery routes, reduce fuel consumption, and improve delivery times.
- **Fleet Management**: Big data enables real-time monitoring of vehicles, providing insights into performance, maintenance needs, and driver behavior, which leads to better fleet management and cost savings.

---

## *Case Studies in Healthcare, Finance, and E-Commerce*

### 1. Healthcare: Predictive Analytics for Patient Care

**Case Study**: A major hospital chain in the U.S. implemented a predictive analytics model to reduce readmissions for heart failure patients. By analyzing patient demographics, medical histories, treatment data, and real-time monitoring of vital signs, the hospital was able to predict which patients were at high risk of readmission.

- **Results**: The predictive model helped healthcare providers intervene early, providing more targeted care and reducing readmission rates by 15%. This not only improved patient outcomes but also saved the hospital millions in avoidable readmission costs.

## 2. Finance: Fraud Detection in Real-Time

**Case Study**: A global bank implemented a big data-driven fraud detection system to analyze millions of transactions in real time. Using machine learning algorithms, the bank was able to detect fraudulent activities as soon as they occurred by analyzing transaction patterns and comparing them with historical data.

- **Results**: The system identified fraudulent transactions within seconds, reducing fraud-related losses by 30%. It also minimized false positives, ensuring legitimate transactions were not unnecessarily flagged.

## 3. E-Commerce: Personalization and Customer Engagement

**Case Study**: An e-commerce giant used big data analytics to personalize the shopping experience for millions of users. By analyzing customer behavior, search history, purchase history, and demographic data, the company implemented a recommendation system that suggested products tailored to individual preferences.

- **Results**: The personalized recommendations led to a 25% increase in average order value and a 20% increase in customer retention. This demonstrates how big data can drive sales and improve customer loyalty by providing more relevant experiences.

---

## The Impact of Big Data on Society and the Economy

Big data is having profound implications on both society and the economy. It is reshaping industries, driving innovation, and changing the way businesses and governments make decisions.

### 1. Societal Impact

- **Privacy Concerns**: The collection and analysis of personal data by organizations raise important ethical and privacy concerns. Governments, businesses, and individuals must work together to balance the benefits of big data with the need for personal privacy.
- **Job Creation**: Big data is driving the creation of new job opportunities in fields like data science, machine learning, and AI. However, this also necessitates the upskilling of

workers and addressing potential job displacement in traditional sectors.

- **Informed Decision-Making**: Big data allows governments and non-profits to make evidence-based decisions. For example, data analytics can be used to improve public policy, track disease outbreaks, and optimize public transportation systems.

## 2. Economic Impact

- **Business Growth**: Companies leveraging big data gain a competitive advantage by optimizing operations, improving customer engagement, and making data-driven decisions. This can result in higher efficiency, reduced costs, and greater market share.

- **Market Innovation**: Big data is driving innovation by enabling companies to create new products and services that better meet customer needs. In industries like healthcare, transportation, and finance, big data has led to the development of new business models and services.

- **GDP Growth**: Economies that embrace big data are seeing increased productivity and innovation, contributing to overall GDP growth. According to studies, the economic value of big data could add trillions of dollars to the global economy in the coming years.

## *Real-World Example: Big Data in Smart Agriculture*

**Smart agriculture** refers to the use of big data and IoT technologies to improve farming practices, optimize crop yields, and reduce waste. With advancements in sensors, drones, and satellite imaging, farmers can now gather and analyze large datasets to make more informed decisions about crop management, irrigation, and pest control.

### 1. Data Collection in Smart Agriculture

Farmers collect data from various sources:

- **Soil Sensors**: Measure moisture levels, pH, and temperature, allowing for optimized irrigation and fertilization.
- **Weather Data**: Helps predict weather patterns, such as rainfall or temperature fluctuations, which can affect crop growth.
- **Satellite and Drone Imaging**: Provides detailed imagery of crops, helping farmers monitor plant health and detect issues like pest infestations or nutrient deficiencies.

### 2. Data Analysis and Decision-Making

By analyzing data from these sources, farmers can make more precise and timely decisions:

- **Precision Agriculture**: Big data enables farmers to apply fertilizers, water, and pesticides only where needed, reducing waste and optimizing resource use.
- **Yield Prediction**: By analyzing historical weather patterns, soil data, and crop performance, farmers can predict crop yields and plan harvests accordingly.
- **Crop Disease Monitoring**: Drones and satellite imaging allow farmers to detect early signs of disease or pest infestations, enabling quick intervention and minimizing crop loss.

## 3. Results and Benefits

- **Increased Efficiency**: By using data to optimize the use of resources, farmers can increase crop yields while reducing waste and environmental impact.
- **Sustainability**: Smart agriculture practices help conserve water, reduce pesticide use, and minimize carbon emissions, contributing to more sustainable farming.
- **Economic Growth**: Farmers who implement big data technologies can increase productivity, reduce costs, and improve profits, contributing to economic growth in rural areas.

In this chapter, we explored **real-world applications** of big data across industries, with case studies in **healthcare, finance**, and **e-commerce**, showcasing how big data is transforming decision-making, optimizing operations, and driving innovation. We also discussed the **impact of big data** on society and the economy, highlighting both the opportunities and challenges it presents.

Finally, we examined a **real-world example** of how big data is being applied in **smart agriculture** to increase efficiency, sustainability, and profitability. As big data continues to evolve, its potential to transform industries and improve lives will only grow, creating new opportunities for businesses, governments, and individuals alike.

# Chapter 23: Getting Started with Big Data

The world of big data is vast and complex, but with the right tools and guidance, anyone can get started on the journey to harness its potential. Whether you're a beginner or looking to deepen your knowledge, this chapter will provide practical advice on **how to begin working with big data**, introduce essential **tools and resources** for learning big data technologies, and guide you through **building your first big data project**. We will conclude with a **real-world example** of **building a basic big data pipeline** to show how theory turns into practice.

---

### *How to Begin Working with Big Data*

Starting with big data can seem overwhelming, given its scale and complexity. However, by breaking down the process into manageable steps, you can build a strong foundation and start working with big data effectively.

### 1. Understand the Basics of Big Data

Before diving into big data tools and technologies, it's essential to have a solid understanding of the fundamental concepts behind it:

- **Volume, Velocity, and Variety**: Learn the three main characteristics of big data—how it's generated (velocity), how much of it there is (volume), and the different formats it takes (variety).

- **Big Data Architecture**: Familiarize yourself with the basic architecture used in big data systems, including data storage (e.g., Hadoop, NoSQL databases), processing (e.g., Spark, MapReduce), and analysis (e.g., machine learning, data visualization).

- **Data Collection and Preprocessing**: Understand how data is collected, cleaned, and prepared for analysis. This is often the most time-consuming step in the big data workflow.

## 2. Learn the Essential Big Data Tools

Big data relies on specialized tools for storage, processing, and analysis. As a beginner, focus on the most widely used technologies:

- **Hadoop**: A framework that allows for the distributed processing and storage of large datasets across clusters of computers.

- **Apache Spark**: A powerful, fast processing engine that can handle real-time analytics and batch processing.

- **NoSQL Databases**: Learn how non-relational databases, such as MongoDB and Cassandra, handle large volumes of unstructured data.

- **SQL**: While NoSQL databases are critical, many big data projects still use **SQL** for querying structured data, making it an essential tool for big data professionals.

### 3. Start Small and Focus on Real-World Problems

Rather than jumping into large-scale projects, start with small, well-defined tasks that help you understand the basic principles of big data. For example:

- **Analyzing small datasets**: Start by working with small datasets that simulate real-world big data, such as public datasets from sources like Kaggle, UCI Machine Learning Repository, or government open data portals.
- **Personal projects**: Choose a personal project, such as analyzing social media data or weather patterns, to apply big data technologies in a practical way.

By starting small and working on real-world problems, you will gain experience and confidence before tackling larger, more complex datasets.

---

### *Tools and Resources for Learning Big Data Technologies*

There are a wide variety of resources available to help you learn big data technologies. Whether you prefer self-paced online courses, reading books, or joining a community, there is something for every learning style.

### 1. Online Learning Platforms

- **Coursera**: Offers courses and specializations in big data technologies, such as the "Big Data" specialization from the University of California, San Diego, or courses on **Hadoop** and **Apache Spark**.
- **edX**: Provides courses from top universities and organizations, such as **MIT** and **IBM**, covering big data fundamentals and specific tools like **Hadoop**, **NoSQL**, and **data science with big data**.
- **Udemy**: Has a wide selection of affordable courses on specific tools and frameworks, including hands-on tutorials for building big data projects with **Spark**, **Hadoop**, and **Python**.

## 2. Books

Books are a great way to dive deeper into big data technologies and understand both the theory and practical applications. Some popular books for big data beginners include:

- **"Hadoop: The Definitive Guide"** by Tom White – A comprehensive guide to understanding and working with Hadoop, the foundational big data technology.
- **"Spark: The Definitive Guide"** by Bill Chambers and Matei Zaharia – A thorough introduction to Apache Spark, explaining how to leverage its power for big data processing.

- **"Data Science for Business"** by Foster Provost and Tom Fawcett – This book focuses on how big data technologies are applied in real-world business problems.

## 3. Big Data Communities and Forums

Join big data communities to interact with other learners and professionals, ask questions, and stay up to date with the latest trends and developments:

- **Stack Overflow**: Ask questions and get help from the big data community.
- **Reddit**: Subreddits like **r/bigdata** and **r/datascience** offer discussions, resources, and advice on big data technologies.
- **GitHub**: Explore big data projects, contribute to open-source big data tools, and learn from others' code.
- **Kaggle**: A great place to practice with datasets, participate in competitions, and engage with a community of data enthusiasts.

## *Building Your First Big Data Project*

Once you've grasped the basics of big data and familiarized yourself with essential tools, it's time to build your first big data project. This hands-on experience will help you understand how all the components of a big data workflow come together.

## 1. Define Your Problem

Choose a clear, manageable project that uses big data tools to solve a real-world problem. For example:

- **Analyzing traffic patterns**: Use public traffic datasets to analyze congestion patterns and optimize traffic flow.
- **Sentiment analysis**: Scrape social media data to analyze sentiment towards a product or brand.
- **Sales forecasting**: Use historical sales data to build a predictive model that forecasts future sales.

## 2. Collect and Prepare Data

Once you've defined your problem, collect the necessary data. You can use publicly available datasets or gather data from web scraping or APIs. After collecting data, preprocess it to clean and transform it into a usable format. This could involve:

- **Data cleaning**: Handling missing values, removing duplicates, and standardizing data formats.
- **Data transformation**: Aggregating, normalizing, or encoding data for machine learning.

## 3. Choose Your Big Data Tools

For a beginner project, focus on using **Apache Hadoop** for storage and **Apache Spark** for processing. Set up the environment on your local machine or use cloud-based platforms like **Google Cloud Dataproc** or **AWS EMR** for Hadoop and Spark.

### 4. Analyze and Visualize Data

Once your data is ready, begin analyzing it using **SQL**, **Spark**, or **Python**. If your project involves machine learning, use **MLlib** (Spark's machine learning library) or **scikit-learn** to build models. Afterward, visualize your findings using **Tableau**, **Power BI**, or **Matplotlib** in Python.

### 5. Interpret Results and Improve

Analyze your results and iteratively improve your model or analysis. For example, if you're building a predictive model, fine-tune your algorithms, explore new features, and evaluate performance using metrics like accuracy, precision, or F1-score.

---

### *Real-World Example: Building a Basic Big Data Pipeline*

To better understand how big data technologies work together, let's walk through a simple example of building a big data pipeline.

### 1. Problem: Predictive Maintenance for Industrial Equipment

Imagine you work for a manufacturing company that wants to predict when machines will fail. This will help the company schedule maintenance and avoid costly downtime.

### 2. Data Collection

The company installs IoT sensors on each piece of equipment to monitor key variables like temperature, vibration, and pressure. This data is streamed in real-time and collected into a central storage system.

### 3. Data Storage

The sensor data is stored in a **Hadoop Distributed File System (HDFS)** or **NoSQL database** like **MongoDB**, depending on the volume and type of data. For real-time analysis, data may also be stored in **Apache Kafka** streams.

### 4. Data Processing

The data is processed using **Apache Spark**. In this case, you would:

- Use **Spark Streaming** to ingest real-time sensor data.
- Apply data transformation steps like filtering out noisy readings and aggregating data to a more useful format.
- Run machine learning models using **MLlib** to predict the likelihood of machine failure based on the sensor readings.

### 5. Visualization

The results are visualized using a dashboard (e.g., **Power BI** or **Tableau**) to monitor the health of machines in real time. Alerts are sent out when maintenance is needed, and the system is continuously optimized using historical data.

In this chapter, we explored how to get started with **big data**, from understanding the basics and learning the essential tools to building your first project. We discussed the importance of **practical experience** in applying big data technologies to real-world problems and provided a step-by-step guide to building a simple **big data pipeline**.

As you continue your journey with big data, remember that learning is an ongoing process. Keep experimenting with new projects, stay up to date with emerging technologies, and engage with the big data community. By doing so, you'll be well-equipped to tackle complex data challenges and unlock the full potential of big data in any industry.

www.ingramcontent.com/pod-product-compliance
Lightning Source LLC
LaVergne TN
LVHW022340060326
832902LV00022B/4148